The Complete Hang Gliding Guide

Noel Whittall

In the same series:

The Complete Cycle Sport Guide
The Complete Microlight Guide
The Complete Sailing Guide
The Complete Windsurfing Guide

First published 1984
by A & C Black (Publishers) Limited
35 Bedford Row, London, WC1R 4JH,
England

Whittall, Noel
  The complete hang gliding guide.
  1. Hang gliding
  I. Title
  797.5'5   GV764

  ISBN 0-7136-2456-6 Cased
  ISBN 0-7136-2457-4 Paperback

Design: Krystyna Hewitt
Illustrations: Douglas Hewitt

Photographic credits
Michael J. Barry: 66, 111tl
Trevor Birkbeck: 35, 75t, 83, 111b, 131bl
Dundee University: 33
Mainair Sports Ltd: 71t, 72, 73, 74r, 75b, 76, 77
Solar Wings Ltd: 17
Steve Thompson: 58, 59, 66/67, 67
Robert Whittall Jr: 34, 35, 117, 142l
Wiltshire Hang Gliding Centre: 141

The author wishes gratefully to acknowledge
permission to reproduce the photographs
listed above. All other photographs are by
the author.

The co-operation of the British Hang Gliding
Association in giving permission to
reproduce their Pilot 1, 2 and 3 requirements
is also gratefully acknowledged.

Typesetting and origination by
Paul Hicks Limited,
Burrington Way, Plymouth, Devon.

Printed and bound in Great Britain
by A. Wheaton & Co. Ltd, Exeter and London

The Complete
HANG GLIDING
Guide

Noel Whittall

Adam and Charles Black
London

This book is dedicated to the
memory of John Turner. He taught
many of us to fly safely, yet never
appeared to give a lesson.

Contents

A very early English Rogallo. Note lack of top rigging, minimal harness and inefficient sail

Given good conditions, simple gliders could soar quite well, as this picture from 1975 shows

The Skyhook 3A was a typical Rogallo-based glider of 1974–75

1. Introduction

A dozen or so years ago nobody in the world had made flights of more than a few seconds in what we now know as a hang glider. Yet for centuries man had experimented with wings of canvas, linen or silk without ever completely entering that third dimension in which the birds, bats and butterflies move with apparent ease.

It is true that foot-launched aircraft had been made since Queen Victoria's time—full-sized kits were on sale as early as the 1890s—but they invariably suffered from a major design shortcoming: straight line glide performance was acceptable, but directional control was sketchy to put it mildly.

Then, early this century, modern aviation was born when the Wright Brothers and their successors made powered planes work. Exploration of the gliding efficiency of aircraft stopped almost completely, because the key to performance seemed to be the development of bigger and better engines.

Not until well after the 1914–18 war did interest in gliding reappear, when Germany forced glider development ahead. This was a direct result of the limitations imposed on the country, which virtually banned powered aircraft. By a natural progression, these aeroplane-based gliders gradually developed into the sleek and

expensive sailplanes which are a familiar sight at gliding clubs throughout the world, while the ultra-lightweight shoulder-borne wings of the earliest pioneers were all but forgotten.

Certainly a few individuals built foot-launched planes, and occasionally plans appeared in hobby magazines—particularly in the USA—for primitive box-kite type designs. These were usually very complex, very fragile or both, and would-be pilots soon became disheartened.

Then in the 1950s and 1960s two rather dissimilar lines of research led to the first 'Rogallo Kites'

The 'Eagle & Child': simple suspended flight is a dream going back to medieval times

appearing, and around 1970 the evolution of the soon-to-be familiar multi-coloured fabric and aluminium deltas was well under way.

The shape was a direct result of Dr Francis Rogallo's experimental work in the USA. His search for a steerable parachute with a degree of glide performance terminated in what was in effect two shallow semi-cones of fabric joined edge to edge, and held in shape with a simple tubular frame. It was not originally visualised as a sporting machine, and various versions were built, some big enough to lift a Jeep while being towed.

By the mid 1960s, in California, Richard Miller and some student friends were ground skimming on polythene and bamboo Rogallo wings, while hanging by the armpits on a subframe. Control was by swinging the hips and legs, and apparently somewhat vague.

Meanwhile two Australian water-ski showmen, Bill Bennett and Bill Moyes, were making their vital contribution to the new sport. As an additional attraction during their ski-shows, they used flat 'man-carrying' kites towed behind boats. The novelty in these kites was that the flier was suspended from the centre of the framework in a seat like a child's playground swing, while holding on to a bar fitted rigidly to the kite. By moving his whole body he could exert

7

The full battening made this Australian glider very advanced for the period (1976)

reasonable control over the otherwise notoriously unstable flat kites.

So, putting it simply, the Australians had unstable kites with a good control system while the Americans had stable kites with poor control. When the swing seat was first fitted to a Rogallo wing by another Australian, John Dickenson, the practical hang glider had arrived, and generations of inventors rotated in their graves and kicked themselves for missing such a gloriously simple idea.

News of these first practical Rogallo-based gliders strayed across the Atlantic sometime in 1971, and independently but simultaneously Geoff McBroom in Bristol, Len Gabriels in Oldham and Ken Messenger in Marlborough started commercial development of British-made models. A new form of sport aviation had arrived which was available to anyone with a sense of adventure and an earnest desire to fly. Since then the activity has evolved as fast in these islands as anywhere in the world, and our pilots win consistently at international level.

Those of us who started to fly ten or more years ago frequently went through a somewhat bruising experience: there were no schools where we could be taught to fly safely, and little was known about how to trim the gliders we flew. We

could not go and ask an expert how to proceed, because the 'experts' of the day probably only had a couple of weeks more experience than the novices. What little was understood about such vital matters as air turbulence on flying sites had usually been discovered the hard way, and all in all it was surprising there were not more really serious accidents.

Fortunately the picture is now very different. The British Hang Gliding Association has organised the sport properly, and its training

methods are both safe and effective. Gliders are well designed and good communications and research within the sport ensure that the hard lessons learned by the pioneers are available painlessly to one and all.

But if this tempts you into contemplating a start in hang gliding, then beware! You are almost certainly going to change your life. After a couple of days or so at training school you will discover that instead of being clipped into a great awkward

The VJ23 has an extremely good glide performance, but its complexity prevented it becoming popular. Its rigid wing and moveable control surfaces make this a Class 2 hang glider

flapping tent of a kite which seems bent on resisting your every command, you hold it at just the correct angle to both hillside and wind. Then you take those few purposeful running steps exactly as your instructor commanded, and you FLY. The previous teaching all becomes relevant as you glide down the slope before easing the control bar out prior to a stand-up landing. And from that moment on you will always be a hang glider pilot. If you see a hang glider in an advertisement or on TV, you will not think to yourself, 'one day I wouldn't mind trying that'. You will *know* what it feels like. You will probably have become hooked on one of the most magical of sports in which your steadily increasing knowledge of the air, the weather, the countryside, the flight of birds, plus the company of other pilots, will more than compensate for the chills and frustrations inevitably associated with any weather-dependent pursuit.

Can anyone fly a hang glider?

Provided you are sixteen years old you can fly a hang glider in the British Isles. You do not have to be super-fit or particularly gifted in circus skills, but reasonable health and an average sense of balance

An Emu soars the South Downs in 1979. This glider has a bowsprit and extra wires instead of the more normal cross-bars

are necessary. It also helps to have a moderately developed sense of fear and a mature approach to the dangers.

Yes, there is no point in pretending that there is no danger in the sport: danger is inherent in all aspects of sporting aviation. The pilot must at all times be dedicated to avoiding accidents by adopting a positive and permanent attitude to flying safety. Hence the essential need for mental maturity.

The popular press image of the hang glider pilot is of a fearless youth who hurls himself off cliffs while remaining attached to a kite by muscle power alone. Fortunately this is as inaccurate as the other common conviction among the public that we plummet out of the sky the moment the wind stops!

Fliers come from all walks of life and span the age range from student to pensioner. It is true to say that the flying membership of clubs is predominantly male, and I apologise in advance for referring to the pilot as 'he' quite often throughout this text. British women fliers more than compensate for their relatively small numbers by flying to a very high standard at both national and international level. At the time of writing two English girls, Jenny Ganderton and Judy Leden, between them claim every women's international hang gliding record.

The wheels on the bottom bar are essential for safety during basic training

So if you can ride a bicycle and climb a couple of flights of stairs without passing out, then all you need is a modest urge for adventure and you have all the essentials required before signing on for a course of hang gliding lessons. Lessons which may well lead on to your becoming one of the still quite small number of people who have earned the privilege of knowing exactly how it feels to step off a hillside and fly free.

2. The hang glider and basic equipment

By definition, a hang glider is an aircraft which can be foot-launched and landed by the unaided efforts of the pilot. Although its construction is fairly simple and almost all the components are visible, it is truly an aeroplane and must be treated all the time as such.

By far the most common type is the weight-shift controlled, flexible-winged glider derived from the original Rogallo concept. Simple versions are used to train novices, while more refined models are the choice of club and competition pilots. Unless otherwise stated, this family of glider is the type the author has in mind throughout the text. For sheer glide performance it can be beaten by its rigid-winged brothers, but ease of transport, rigging and handling on the ground, coupled with forgiving characteristics in the air, make it the choice of ninety-nine per cent of sporting fliers at present.

How the glider flies

Although a hang glider in its most simple form may appear almost

Above: Carrying up—without airflow over the wings the sail on this type of glider is able to relax into quite a different shape to that which it assumes during flight

Below: First Solo! See how the sail is inflated during flight. Glider: Hiway 'Stubby'

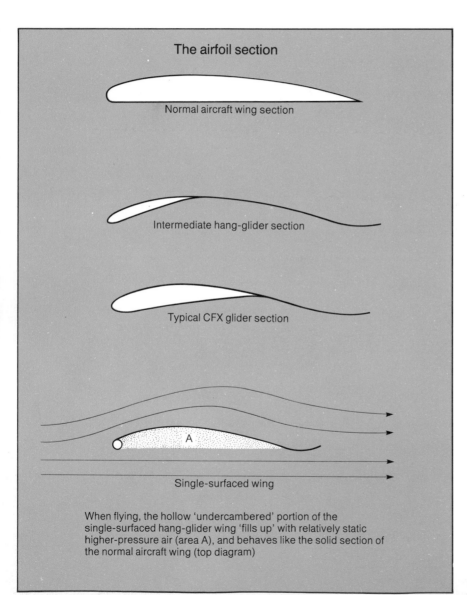

The airfoil section

Normal aircraft wing section

Intermediate hang-glider section

Typical CFX glider section

A

Single-surfaced wing

When flying, the hollow 'undercambered' portion of the single-surfaced hang-glider wing 'fills up' with relatively static higher-pressure air (area A), and behaves like the solid section of the normal aircraft wing (top diagram)

primitive, it remains in the air by exploiting exactly the same physical laws as any other heavier-than-air craft.

The curvature of the wing from front to rear forms an *airfoil section*. When an airfoil is moved through air it has the effect of reducing the air pressure over its upper surface. Naturally the air below then tries to push the wing up into the lower pressure area produced above it, and so *lift* is generated.

This lift is reinforced by arranging for the front edge of the wing—the *leading edge*—to enter the air while inclined slightly upwards. This raises the pressure under the wing still further. This angle at which the wing advances is called the *angle of attack*.

The propulsive force which keeps all gliders moving through the air is gravity. As a means of driving an aircraft it has the merit of being totally reliable: unfortunately it functions only in a downward direction. The skill of the glider designer lies in producing a wing which develops as much lift as possible over an acceptably wide range of speed, so that the disadvantage of having an 'engine' which only works downwards is minimised. In Chapter 5 we deal with the art of fooling the machine into climbing by flying it in air which is moving upwards faster than the glider is going downwards.

Airspeed and stalling

Your wing will have to develop enough lift to support the combined weight of glider and pilot. We have mentioned that the airfoil plays a vital part in generating this lift by lowering the pressure above the wing. It will help new pilots to fly their gliders more safely if they have some understanding of exactly how and why this happens and how the air behaves while it is happening.

Imagine the leading edge advancing through the air. It meets a particular chunk of air and splits it horizontally. The air rather resents this treatment and would like to reunite at the earliest opportunity. This it cannot do until the wing has passed completely. What is more, because of the cunning shape of the airfoil, that portion of air which found itself on top of the wing discovers that it has a longer path to travel than its more fortunate mate below. As it has only the same amount of time to travel this longer route, it has to hurry. When air (or any other gas or fluid for that matter) speeds up, its pressure decreases. So as long as the wing keeps splitting fresh chunks of air, and as long as that air travels in an orderly manner over the wing, then the pressure above the wing is lower than that below and consistent lift is developed.

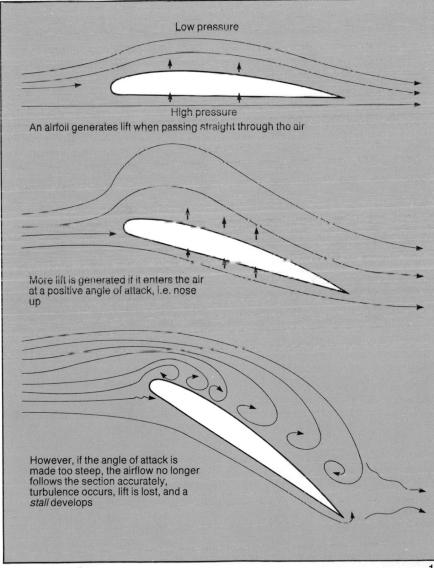

Low pressure

High pressure

An airfoil generates lift when passing straight through the air

More lift is generated if it enters the air at a positive angle of attack, i.e. nose up

However, if the angle of attack is made too steep, the airflow no longer follows the section accurately, turbulence occurs, lift is lost, and a *stall* develops

The stall

It is when the air is provoked into behaving in a disorderly manner that the problems start. If you attempt to generate more lift by flying at too steep an angle of attack, the air above the wing will find it is unable to follow closely the upper contour of the airfoil. It abandons any idea of reuniting with the portion it was next to before the leading edge came along, and degenerates into an undisciplined rabble towards the back of the wing. Some of the under-wing air also nips up around the trailing edge to join in, and the pressure difference is lost. With that goes the lift: the wing is *stalled*, and from that moment the pilot is no longer in control until the orderly airflow is restored. The only way to do this is by reducing the angle of attack which increases the speed. However, it also involves losing quite a lot of height, and all hang glider pilots must understand both the cause and effect of stalling, and avoid letting it happen except under controlled conditions with plenty of altitude to spare.

Glider performance

The closer we look at a hang glider, the more we find that it embodies a mass of compromises. A satisfactory glider must have the right blend of *glide ratio*, *minimum sink rate*, *stalling speed*, *stability* and *handling*. It must also be built so strongly that there is no chance of any part of it failing even when exposed to the most severe flying conditions, and yet be sufficiently light to be easily carried by the pilot alone.

Glide ratio

This is the ratio of the distance that the glider travels over the ground relative to a given loss of height. A training glider will have a ratio of about 6:1. For every six feet it flies forwards in still air, it will lose one foot of height. The more sleek double-surfaced high-performance machines will achieve a ratio in the region of 10:1 or even 12:1.

This improved ratio is achieved mainly because the advanced glider generates less drag and has a more efficient airfoil section than its training counterpart. Rather conveniently, the glide ratio turns out to be the same as the ratio of lift developed by the wing against the drag generated by the passage of the glider and pilot through the air. Because the glider is flying and not dropping out of the sky like a dead sparrow, we can work out that the wing must be generating the same amount of lift as its all-up weight plus pilot. Typically this would be about 240 lb. The total drag in this case would be 24 lb for a 10:1 glider or $\frac{240}{6} = 40$ lb for the less efficient training model.

Drag

Having raised the ugly subject of drag, we may as well get to grips with the notion that there are actually two different types. The most easily visualised is *profile drag*. This is the spoon-through-treacle type, and gets greater the faster you go, as anyone who has ever stuck a hand out of a car window at different speeds will appreciate. More subtle is *induced drag*, so called because the action of the wing generating lift also induces drag. Most of this is due to confused air at the wingtip areas which flows outwards and then eddies around the tips before being left behind in the form of spiral vortices. It is at its most pronounced at low speeds and high angles of attack. As the speed goes up, so does the efficiency of the wing, which in turn lowers the induced drag.

Of course, the overall drag figure is the one which influences performance. The best glide angle will therefore be found at the speed where the two drag figures (profile and induced) added together are smallest. Admittedly you will not be able to work it out for any given glider without having a vast amount of time and patience, but it is valuable to appreciate that there is only one airspeed for the craft you are flying which will deliver the best glide performance.

Minimum sink

Usually abbreviated to *min-sink*, this is the smallest rate of height loss achievable by your glider. It occurs at a slow flying speed—usually not far above stalling speed—and is most clearly observed when ridge soaring in smooth conditions. Gliders which are not renowned for high speed performance will often fly just as high as the 'hot ships' in the ridge lift, as long as the wind does not become so strong that they have to travel faster than their min-sink speed in order to stay in the lift band.

Stalling speed

As explained earlier, a wing can stall at any speed if the angle of attack is too great. However, when hang glider pilots talk of stalling speed they usually mean minimum stalling speed, which is self-explanatory. There is a speed below which the wing just will not pass through enough air to generate sufficient lift to keep it flying. The airflow over it separates and becomes turbulent, and the wing starts to drop. According to the design of glider the drop may be quite sudden or a relatively gentle 'mushing'. It will always be preceded by a loss of lateral control. Because the minimum stall speed is probably only a mile an hour or so less than the minimum sink speed on the

average hang glider, the new pilot must be constantly on guard against flying too slowly and straying into the dangerous area of the stall speed.

Washout

The stalling characteristics of your glider are influenced by the amount of washout in the wing. As many of the photographs show, there is a form of twist throughout each wing

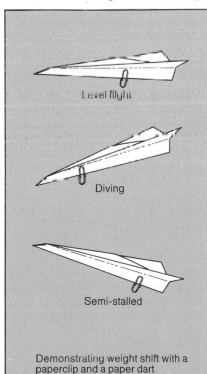

Level flight

Diving

Semi-stalled

Demonstrating weight shift with a paperclip and a paper dart

which allows the centre sections to fly at a much higher angle of attack than the tips. This reduction in the tip angle is called washout, and ensures that as the glider is slowed down the stall develops progressively from centre to tip. It does not require a vivid imagination to see that a glider in which the tips stall easily will be most unpleasant and dangerous to fly, because a stalled tip drops rapidly. There are many occasions when one tip is flying faster than the other—in turns for example, or when ridge soaring in the wind gradient close to a hill, and the pilot needs as much warning as possible of an impending stall. A vicious drop of a wingtip does not qualify.

Control

It is not sufficient to make a wing which will fly. That is really not particularly difficult. The clever part lies in controlling the wing in the differing conditions in which it will find itself.

The system we use on most hang gliders is *weight shift*. The pilot swings in his harness from the centre of gravity of the wing and by moving his weight relative to the glider, changes its attitude. Pulling forward reduces the angle of attack, thus speeding up the aircraft. If he moves far enough forward the glider will dive. Pushing his body backwards slows the wing and may

15

eventually stall it. A few minutes of experiment with a paper dart and a paperclip representing the pilot will demonstrate this effect very clearly.

Control in roll is rather more subtle. Put in its simplest form the pilot moves right to turn right and so on. However, simply moving across the bar is not enough—it merely serves to initiate a spiral dive which is not exactly what the flier usually has in mind. If we look at what happens to the glider in a turn, then the problem and the solution will be seen.

As the pilot moves his weight sideways, he places extra load on the wing on the side to which he moves. Because the whole airframe is flexible to a certain extent, more billow is introduced into the loaded wing, which makes it slightly less efficient than the other one which has simultaneously tightened a little. This tighter wing develops more lift than one with extra billow, and so naturally it tries to fly higher. The net effect is that the glider starts to roll. Only the presence of either generous billow, a deep keel pocket, or a fin prevents it from sideslipping at the same time.

So we now have a glider which is flying with one wing higher than the other but still almost in a straight line. To make it really carve into the turn, all the pilot needs to do is to move his weight back by pushing on the control bar. In level flight this would just move the nose up and slow the glider, but remember, it is banked over now, and consequently the nose leads the whole machine into a turn in the direction of the bank.

Of course, *airspeed* is all-important in turns. The minimum stalling speed increases rapidly in relation to the angle of bank, and if the turn is initiated at too slow a speed, the act of pushing out on the bar will result in a vicious stall and very little else. More about turns appears in the chapter on Soaring.

Handling and stability

Our glider must have reasonable stability in three axes: pitch, roll and yaw.

Pitch stability
For pitch stability, the wing section is provided with *reflex* at the rear. This ensures that the nose cannot drop too low in flight and become stabilised in a dive.

Roll stability
Roll stability comes about because the wings are usually provided with a little *dihedral* which has an aerodynamic self-levelling effect.

Yaw stability
Yaw stability is what prevents the machine flying crabwise. It is taken care of by the presence of side area from fin, keelpocket etc, and because of *sweepback*, which has the same effect on yaw as that which dihedral has on roll.

Of course, the whole glider stays the right way up largely because of the pendular stability contributed by the pilot's weight, which keeps the overall centre of gravity well below the wing.

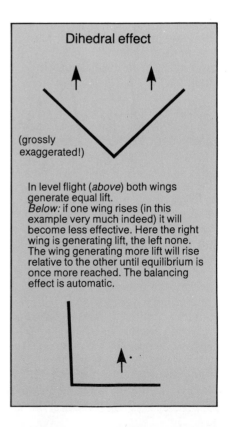

Dihedral effect

(grossly exaggerated!)

In level flight (*above*) both wings generate equal lift.
Below: if one wing rises (in this example very much indeed) it will become less effective. Here the right wing is generating lift, the left none. The wing generating more lift will rise relative to the other until equilibrium is once more reached. The balancing effect is automatic.

A static test of airframe strength. The glider is suspended just clear of the ground while ballast equivalent to at least six times the normal all-up weight is added

Construction

The first hang gliders were made of any materials which came to hand—bamboo carpet poles, polythene sheet, t.v. aerial tubing, rope and coach bolts. Fortunately the motto of the time was 'low and slow', and the foremost magazine about the sport was called *Groundskimmer*.

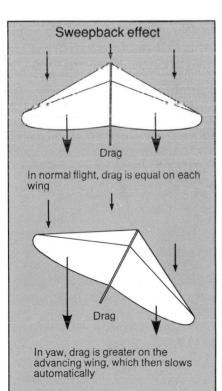

Sweepback effect

Drag

In normal flight, drag is equal on each wing

Drag

In yaw, drag is greater on the advancing wing, which then slows automatically

All that has now changed. Your aircraft will have a framework of high tensile aluminium tubing formed by a most specialised process and given a corrosion-resistant anodised surface. The nuts and bolts will be aircraft quality, and the sailcloth heavy-duty Terylene or Dacron. It will be strong enough to endure at least six times its normal positive loading and three times the negative loading without breaking up. If you have picked a model from a reputable manufacturer who has sought the BHGA seal of approval, you can also be assured that it possesses safe flying characteristics. To pass the BHGA's tests it must not show any problems with instability, dive recovery or spinning tendencies.

Basic equipment

It is going to be cold out on the hills exposed to the wind, and you will need the right clothing if your flying days are not to be an ordeal.

Your requirements will change slightly as your flying skills develop. Early on you spend more time foot slogging than flying, and strong waterproof boots and clothing which can 'breathe' are the main essentials, plus of course a crash helmet which fits well and is comfortable. Leather gloves are another must, padded ski-type for winter, thin in summer.

Boots
Boots need to give some ankle support, particularly at the learning stage, but beware of the type which use hooks around which to run the laces. These have been known to engage with the rear flying wires of the glider during flight, which of course prevents the pilot weight shifting effectively. At least one fatal accident has been due to this, so hooked boots are to be avoided at all costs.

Helmet
Many hang gliding accidents are relatively minor affairs of the 'stumble and fall' variety. It is by no means unusual for the pilot's head to contact the airframe during these, and then the helmet suddenly becomes far from ornamental. A minor bang with a good helmet could well be a cracked skull without.

How *not* to engage the stirrup: the pilot is not concentrating on flying speed. Glider: Hiway Scorpion

The actual type of helmet is a personal choice, and provided it is up to the U.S. Snell Z90 standard or BSI 5361 it will be adequate. Bear in mind that your helmet will probably have been produced for a motorcyclist who normally sits fairly vertical: if it is too low at the base of the neck, the prone hang glider pilot may find that the front is pushed down over the eyes!

The main difference between motorcycle helmets and those produced specifically for hang gliding is that the ears are exposed, as many fliers find it easier to judge airspeed if they can hear the wind whistling past.

Harness

In the first years of modern hang gliding the seated harness was normal. However, before very long a few pilots tried lying prone in an effort to reduce drag.

For a few years the two systems continued side by side, but now it is usual to fly semi-prone from the start.

The harness is usually in the form of a padded apron with leg-loops and an arrangement of shoulder and body straps which connect at the suspension point on the glider. Below the apron a cord on each side connects to a stirrup which the pilot engages both to tension the apron in flight and to support his feet.

Variations abound, commonest being the 'cocoon' which extends the apron all the way to the stirrup, and the 'knee hanger' which supports the legs via loops velcroed around the knees.

The karabiner

This is the vital link between the glider and your harness. It is usually made out of high-tensile alloy, and will have its strength marked on it. Your life depends upon your karabiner, so it is not an item upon which to economise. Go for a top quality make, with a locking device—usually a screwed sleeve. The exception to this rule is where you are soaring coastal sites. If there is the remotest chance of your flight finishing in water, then fly with a non-locking karabiner—you will need to get unclipped really fast in water to avoid drowning.

The trainee pilot will find that all the necessary equipment except for warm clothing is provided by the school. However, he should always inspect it personally and understand it, thus establishing good habits which will last throughout his flying career.

3. Learning to fly

There is now only one way to learn the skills of piloting a hang glider: take a course of lessons at a school offering a high standard of instruction. Such a school may be identified by selecting from a list of those registered by the BHGA, which employs a permanent Training Officer whose main job it is to inspect the schools and see that the standards required by the association are maintained.

However, be alive to the risks involved in one or two of the 'alternatives' you may be tempted by:

1 Non-approved or de-registered schools

Potentially risky. Schools are not de-registered without good reason. Maybe their teaching methods are unsound or outdated. Maybe their training sites are excessively hazardous, or their accident rate unacceptably high. Possibly they do not have suitable insurance. At the threshold of your flying career you are in no position to judge, so play safe and go to a registered establishment.

2 The 'bargain glider' with free training thrown in

The worst bargain of all. The plot usually goes along these lines: you announce to a group of friends in the pub that you have at last decided to take up hang gliding. At

First-day students are introduced to the training glider

Inserting the battens

learned to fly, and never take lessons from a failed amateur!

At the training school

Once you have decided on a school, do try and book a full week of lessons. Pupils who do this generally progress with far fewer setbacks than when the course is spread over many weekends. The enemy to rapid progress is the weather, so do be prepared for some disappointments along the way. The range of wind conditions in which the student can safely learn is very limited, so do not get too disheartened if the instructor says 'no flying' when the day looks fine to you. The instructor knows best, and in hang gliding nearly right is not right enough.

Let us follow pupils through a typical school course; just for a change we will allow the weather to be fairly co-operative for a week, during which some of our recruits turn from groundlings into the owners of a Pilot One Hang Gliding Certificate, or P1 for short.

Day 1—a.m.
Blue skies and light wind, and the apprehensive bunch of novices are surprised to find themselves being whisked out to a shallow training hill within ten minutes of signing on. Gliders are on the roof of the minibus although the course

Preparing to rig a training glider

prospectus said that the start was a two-hour introductory lecture. This turns out to be practical lesson one: always use the weather to your advantage. Because conditions are fine and dry and not too windy, ground handling and glider familiarisation are to take precedence over theory.

On the top of the slope the gliders are assembled by the students with guidance from the instructors. With no more than six pupils per group, they find the assembly surprisingly easy and absorb essentials, such as always rigging with the nose of the aircraft pointing into the wind, without much conscious effort. The gliders are bigger than some of the students

once a member of the group you know less well than the others says 'My brother/uncle/neighbour/ boss/lodger has one of those which he doesn't use now—I am sure he would let it go cheap.' If the warning bells do not immediately ring, you will find yourself being shown an ancient glider dragged out from the rafters of a slightly damp garage. All the aluminium framework will have a patina of greying oxide over it with the exception of one control frame side which will look newer than the rest. The brother/uncle/neighbour/ boss/lodger will have a slight but persistent limp and explain that he has now taken up board sailing because his wife prefers it, but he will give you a few lessons with the glider at no extra charge. This is the point at which to make your excuses and leave. Golden rule: never buy any glider until you have

why the training wings are not as sleek-looking as most of those flown by clubmen on the hill. To start on the more advanced gliders would be like learning to drive on a thoroughbred sports car.

Then comes a lesson which is to be a recurring theme throughout training right up to the level of advanced soaring: correct airspeed is vital. The dangers of stalling are naturally stressed in this part of the talk, and the final time is spent on the importance of landing into wind and methods of assessing drift in order to achieve this.

The pupils are given course

Before every flight there must be a check to see that the harness isn't twisted.

had expected, and they learn that brute strength is no substitute for technique and knack when it comes to ground handling the wings and lifting them onto the shoulders for the takeoff position.

Then the pupils try on the training harnesses and practise clipping in and hanging in the control frame.

By the end of the morning's session the group has a good idea of how to rig the training glider, what its various unfamiliar parts are called, how it can become very unruly if held at a wrong angle to the wind, but how it almost magically transforms itself from a deadweight into a powerful lifting force when the angles are correct. To demonstrate this last lesson the pupils are 'flown'

in the glider as the instructors hold onto the bottom rigging wires and run into wind. Finally an instructor flies down the hill, quite probably letting go of the control bar on the way: this is not an act of daredevil nonchalance, but is designed to demonstrate to the pupils that the glider is quite stable and will not plunge to the ground the moment the pilot's grip is relaxed.

Day 1—p.m.
Now comes the promised first lecture.

At this school a short video film introduces the sport, and then an instructor talks about the stages of development which have led to the modern gliders—and also explains

Pupils sometimes find difficulty in waiting for just the correct moment to launch. Eagerness must always be tempered with discretion at all stages of learning

Starting the run: the pilot's shoulders and upper arms feed power progressively into the wing. Any attempt to 'snatch' the glider too fiercely will result in the nose rising and a loss of pitch control

notes and their BHGA information packs which look much less mysterious now that they have had a day in contact with real hang gliders.

The wing is lifting well. One more step to takeoff

Day 2—All day
Straight out to the hill, where the students find themselves being asked for their opinions of the wind and weather conditions. The sport is one in which personal judgement is always essential, so the instructors use the 'question and answer' technique all the time.

The wind is steady at about 10 mph straight onto the slope, so the students are to start on tethered flying. Ropes about 30 feet (10 metres) long are attached to the nose and outer ends of the crossbooms of the gliders, and after all the regular pre-flight inspections and hang checks the first pupil clips in while two others, suitably briefed, take hold of the side tethers. Then, with the instructor on the nose

The pupil is at last airborne. The instructor controls the nose angle during these early flights

tether, a start is made from a little way up the hill. During these early hops the student will never fly higher than five or six feet (1.5–2 m) above the ground, and the instructor will be augmenting the pilots' efforts by judicious tension on the nose rope or pressure on the bottom rigging. Each pupil will probably make three flights in a row, before taking a turn on the side-tethers or a well earned rest.

The forgiving flying characteristics of the training gliders, plus the wheels on the control-bar, ensure that even the students who forget to 'lower the undercarriage' in time for landing do not come to any harm. By lunchtime, all members of the class

Much attention must be given to achieving the correct glide angle (1) before flaring out (2) to slow down enough for a safe touchdown (3)

Careful packing of the glider pays dividends in lengthening its life. The sail must be rolled carefully (1/2), the cables untangled (3), free of kinks (4) and stowed in position (5). Sail ties (6) plus a little strategic padding (7) finish off the job

1

2

3

4

5

6

7

have executed a perfect launch, controlled the airspeed correctly during flight, and performed a stand-up landing. The afternoon is spent trying to assemble all these elements into a single flight!

As the wind dies down towards the end of the day, the tether people have to run faster and faster to keep up with the gliders, and it comes as a great relief when one or two of the group are assessed to be good enough to fly with only the untiring instructor in attendance on the nose rope.

On the way home the group drive past a site at the bottom of which a couple of hang gliders are being de-rigged. The hill looks enormous and vertical, and none of the students can really believe that, weather permitting, there is a fair chance some of them will be making their final Pilot One qualifying flights from the top before the week is out.

Day 3
The wind direction is slightly different today, and instead of going to the small training slope, the group find themselves at the bottom of the hill they had viewed the evening before. After a couple of check flights with the tethers from a launch point a short distance up the hill, all the group fly solo and become increasingly confident. The instructor ties a rope to the kingpost at first, as one or two are having

A trainee learns to weight shift sideways to compensate for drift. Glider: Flexiform 'Spirit'

trouble co-ordinating the landing flare, and a gentle tug at the correct moment as he runs behind the glider soon shows the pupil when to push out, as well as saving a nose-in.

So far all the flying has been virtually straight, with only moderate compensation for drift, but the afternoon session is quite different. The gliders are carried to the top of the hill where the wind is considerably stronger—about 18 mph—and one of the instructors gives a brief demonstration of

soaring, maintaining height with ease and then top-landing. Then the tethers are tied on yet again and after a further briefing, the pupils try tethered soaring. In the strong wind the glider will rise easily, and is allowed to remain about 15 ft up while the pupil pilot practises roll input and turns. He easily grasps the essentials of the difference between airspeed and groundspeed, but the strength and buffeting of the wind plus the unaccustomed height from the valley floor make all the novices

glad the tethers are still in use for this exercise!

Day 4

The wind is still on the 'big site', and it is back to solo flights from part way up the hill. This time the part way gradually moves higher and higher until there is no doubt that the group are steadily accumulating some of the fifteen solo flights with a ground clearance of at least 40 ft required as part of Pilot One qualification.

Just when it is all beginning to

feel easy to some of the pupils, the
instructor places a windsock off to
one side at the bottom of the hill,
and requires the pilots to land in line
with it. This requires a gentle 'S'
turn on the way down, and a few
crosswind landings demonstrate
that even the most confident still
have a fair way to go.

Day 5
A change of wind means driving
some way to a distant site. This is
steeper and not quite as smooth as
the previous one, and the first
flights are 'straight out and down'
again. The wind at the bottom of the
hill is slightly crossed, and the
instructors stress the importance of
monitoring this and landing
correctly into it. A large gulley in the
hillside gives the class their first

Carrying back up again is an inescapable part
of the learning process

The log books must be filled in while the lessons are still fresh in everyone's mind

experience of a really dramatic increase in height as the ground falls steeply away, and also their first local turbulence to cope with. All goes well, but the pupils' increasing proficiency means that as each flight becomes longer, so does the slog back up the hill. By now all the class want to be in the air as much as possible!

At the end of the day the pupils

are making well co-ordinated turns, adjusting airspeed in gusts properly, and the top of the hill does not seem quite as impossible after all.'

Day 6
It is back to the big hill, but more than halfway up this time. The wind is fairly strong—14 mph—and so the 'straps tight' takeoff method is used by all the class for the first

time. The landing mark is very well offset, first to one side and then the other, requiring the turns in the flight path to be quite sharp. Towards the end of the day the chief instructor singles out a couple of the pupils who have done the tidiest turns and together they take one of the gliders to the top of the hill. There is only time for one flight, so a coin is tossed and after a careful briefing the lucky pilot launches from 250 ft above the landing field and that evening enters his first flight of over one minute in his logbook. It may not sound very long, but few minutes in his life will be as sweet. The day ends with a short talk and a simple test paper on flying rules, weather and basic aerodynamics. This is intended to check that the pupils do know things, not to catch them out.

Day 7
By extraordinary good fortune, and quite contrary to the normal weather luck which usually afflicts hang gliding, it is a perfect day. Windspeed is 8–10 mph on top of the big hill, and after being briefed on the landing approach the whole class drive to the top via a road at the back. Satisfied the conditions really are suitably smooth, the instructors supervise the launching and retrieving of one pupil after another until the entire group have had two flights each from the top.

Dry-mouth time comes at the briefing for the third flight: an extra feature is to be stall recovery. All the flying so far has concentrated on avoiding stalling at all costs, yet this time it has to be done deliberately! The briefing is simple: fly straight out from the hill, then push out steadily and firmly until the glider wallows and feels as if it will not respond. Then just as the nose begins to drop, pull on until flying speed is regained. It really is simple enough, and these training gliders are so forgiving that at most 20ft of height is lost during the whole process. Even so, a couple of the pupils cannot bring themselves to slow down enough when it comes to it.

Back at the school, all the pupils except the two non-stallers are given the precious P1 certificates. They are now in a position to really learn about hang gliding, for the learning process never stops. As P1s they can buy a glider themselves, and have enough knowledge to start to get the best out of it. Some of them will carry on through the Pilot rating scheme to P2 and P3. In a few months time they will drive past the big hill after a day soaring a thousand-foot ridge and wonder how it could ever have looked so daunting.

There is much more to learn, but it does not have to be done all at once

The aircraft in the bag, the class clear the hill. Hang glider fliers pride themselves on keeping their sites free of litter

Summary of pilot one requirements

1 Demonstrate correct rigging and pre-flight inspection of hang glider and harness.

2 Fly 15 solo flights with a ground clearance of at least 40 ft (12 m).

3 During each of the three final qualifying flights, execute correctly:

a: unassisted takeoffs.

b: flying a planned flight path, with 90° turns to left and right.

c: stand-up landings in a pre-designated area. These final flights must have a ground clearance of at least 100 ft (30 m), and launch point must be not less than 200 ft (60 m) above the landing area. On the final flight proper recovery from a mild stall must be demonstrated.

4 Show an ability to fly safely in steady winds of up to 18 kts (21 mph) and in gusty conditions of up to 10 kts (12 mph) where the wind speed variation does not exceed 6 kts (7 mph).

Another really good attacking launch. Glider: Hiway Super Scorpion C

5 Pass the BHGA test paper covering the code of good practice, flying rules and recommendations and the student syllabus.

6 Finally, the instructor must be satisfied that the student is of a required standard of airmanship to continue flying training safely and competently.

4. Flying weather

Wind and the atmosphere

'Weather' means slightly different things to different people, but initially hang glider pilots tend to be largely preoccupied with wind strength and direction. The corny old description of wind as 'air in a hurry' is not far from the truth, so it will be helpful to understand some of the reasons why it moves about.

We are only concerned with the behaviour of the air up to about 20,000 ft from the Earth's surface.

This is well within the confines of the Troposphere—the layer of atmosphere nearest to us—where the air behaves in a tolerably consistent and predictable manner.

With suitable clothing flying can continue throughout the year, as this winter shot in Yorkshire shows. Glider: La Mouette 'Azur'

Our air is a mixture of gases, and it shows exactly the same quirks of behaviour gases always had in those dimly-remembered school physics lessons. Quite simply, the density of a gas is affected directly by pressure and heat: the more it is compressed the more dense it becomes, but the more it is heated the less dense it will be. Naturally the densest layer of the air is that nearest the Earth's surface, because it has the weight of all the rest of the atmosphere bearing down upon it, courtesy of our old enemy the force of gravity. If that was the end of the story, the air would be about as active as the sausagemeat layer around yesterday's scotch egg, and gliding would always be a nil-wind flight downhill.

Fortunately, the ability of the air to reduce its density as it warms up, coupled with a reliable but intermittent heat source in the form of the sun, ensures that the atmosphere is constantly active: a perpetual turmoil of molecules rushing about en masse from high pressure to low, bumping into each other and everything else, rising up, sinking down, but almost never staying still!

It is a little ironic that the transparency of air, which makes it very difficult for us to see what it is doing, is responsible for its dynamism. The sun's rays pass right through it without giving up much of their heat. When they hit the Earth's surface it is a different matter—the heat is absorbed, the Earth warms up and in turn conducts heat to the layer of air in contact with it. So the transparency allows the air to warm from the bottom upwards. Remember, though, the bottom layer was also the densest, but now the parts of the layer over the warmer parts of the Earth will be a bit less dense—so they float upwards while heavier, cooler chunks slide in to take their place. When you think about all the different reasons why the Earth heats unevenly—day/night, pole/equator, cloud cover etc, (clouds reflect most of the sun's energy back into space) then it is easy to see why the density is frequently changing, and the air is thereby on the move.

On a global scale we know that the Earth is coldest at the poles and warmest at the equator, so it would appear reasonable to expect an overall constant flow of dense air from the poles towards the equator. Fortunately we are spared the resulting polar blasts 365 days a year because the flow is complicated out of all recognition thanks to the gargantuan swirls induced by the air descending onto a rapidly revolving sphere. These complications are due to 'coriolis effect', a useful expression to drop into conversation from time to time.

Within the global movements there exists an infinity of smaller influences which stir the air up still further: the sunny side of a valley warms up much more than the shady one; the land heats more quickly than the sea; a dark coloured field absorbs more heat than a light one and so on and on.

As a final complication, the composition of the air does not remain constant. There is a wild card in the form of water vapour. The atmosphere can absorb up to just short of 3% of its mass as water vapour. This is lighter than air and so reduces the local atmospheric density. The amount of vapour which can be supported varies according to temperature—the warmer the air, the higher the percentage of vapour which may be absorbed before the air is 'saturated'. Naturally this lighter moist air rises. As it rises it cools, and when cooler can support less water vapour. Condensation then takes place, and the result is visible in the form of cloud and rain. Air passing over an ocean naturally becomes more moist than that which has travelled over a dry land mass.

So, we have the air constantly on the move, travelling in huge swirling patterns and rising up or sinking down according to how warm, cool or damp it is. The results are areas

The anti-clockwise airflow around a depression shows clearly in this satellite shot

of differing pressure, plus interfaces between masses of relatively warm and cool air.

The wind does behave in one quite disciplined fashion: in the northern hemisphere it almost always rotates around a low pressure area in an anti-clockwise direction, and clockwise around a high. South of the equator precisely the opposite rule applies. As the weather in the British Isles is dominated by a progression of low pressure systems (cyclones) originating out in the Atlantic, it is often quite easy to predict the wind direction with reasonable accuracy. Regular viewing of the TV charts helps to show how the patterns develop throughout the week.

Of course, wind direction is not everything for the flier: strength, visibility and rain are important too. Again the TV charts are useful, particularly if you have learned enough about weather to add your own interpretation to them. Enthusiastic fliers will want to read specialist books on the subject, but here are a few overall simplifications which form a basis upon which to build:

Millibars (mb)

Millibars are the unit of measurement for air pressure, and extremes from approximately 870 mb to 1080 mb at sea level have been recorded. For the calibration of instruments, 'standard' pressure of 1013.2 mb is used—this is also the pressure to which all aircraft altimeters are set when flying above 3,000 ft.

Overall, air will try to flow from high to low pressure areas.

Isobars
Isobars are lines connecting points of equal pressure. They are the contour lines of low and high pressure areas. The closer they are together, the stronger the associated winds will probably be.

Fronts
Fronts are the boundaries between air masses of different temperature. They tend to travel according to the same rules as winds around depressions etc., and their passage brings changes in the weather.

Warm fronts
Warm fronts ride up over the colder air and as the warmer moister air rises and cools, the water vapour within it cools, condenses and then rain is almost inevitable. Typical warm fronts usually pass any given point in the British Isles in between four and five hours, so a wet morning does not necessarily mean the afternoon will be unflyable.

Cold fronts
Cold fronts travel more quickly than warm ones, and form a wedge

The pilot is sure to encounter turbulence if he lets this storm come any closer

under the warmer air which is again forced up, bringing storms and rain. However, conditions after the front has passed are often fine, although the resulting unstable air may well be turbulent.

Cyclones
Cyclones are low pressure areas around which the wind usually travels in an anti-clockwise direction in the northern hemisphere.

Anti-cyclones
Anti-cyclones are high pressure systems around which the wind usually blows clockwise.

Troughs
A trough is an elongated low pressure area often associated with frontal movement.

Cols
A col is the temporarily calm area between two active lows or highs.

Top left: High cumulus forming in 'streets' show perfect soaring weather in California

Below left: Forming cumulus in the Yorkshire Dales

The blackness of these cumulus mean that the pilot should be alive to the danger of them developing into cumulo-nimbus

The lapse rate

The lapse rate is the amount by which air temperature drops with height. It varies according to the amount of water vapour present.

Dry air cools at a constant rate of 5.4F° per 1,000 ft (1C° per 100 metres) which is a good enough reason to wrap up if soaring is likely, even though completely dry air is unknown in the British Isles. We are talking here of the **adiabatic** lapse rate: in other words, the temperature reduction is entirely due to the air expanding as it goes higher, because its pressure reduces. The adiabatic lapse rate becomes less when there is water vapour present, and is then no longer constant.

Stable air

Stable air, put simply, is air in which the temperature drop with height is low. Thermal development will therefore be slight and vertical airflows small.

Unstable air

Unstable air is that in which there is a considerable temperature drop with height, i.e. a high lapse rate. A blob of warmed air will remain buoyant to a greater height in such conditions.

Thermals

Thermals are rising bubbles or columns of warmer air which are caused by the ground heating unevenly. They are the usual source of lift for cross-country hang glider flights.

Clouds

Clouds are visible water in the atmosphere, and are an invaluable guide for fliers. As your hang gliding career progresses you will automatically learn to identify clouds and know which are friendly and which are not.

Cumulo-nimbus developing and building rapidly

Cloud types

Cumulus are the favourites: these are the cottonwool-like tufts which so often characterise our summer days. Each cumulus marks the top of a thermal and its appearance can be a guide to its age. If the cloud is fluffy the thermal is probably still active. If ragged, then the thermal is probably spent, and the cloud is said to be decaying. The base of classic cumulus clouds is usually

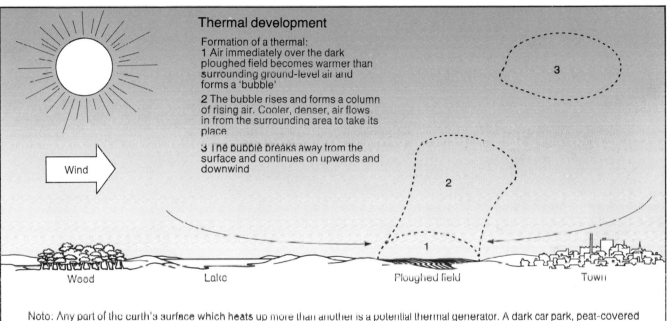

Thermal development

Formation of a thermal:

1 Air immediately over the dark ploughed field becomes warmer than surrounding ground-level air and forms a 'bubble'

2 The bubble rises and forms a column of rising air. Cooler, denser, air flows in from the surrounding area to take its place

3 The bubble breaks away from the surface and continues on upwards and downwind

Wind

Wood   Lake   Ploughed field   Town

Note: Any part of the earth's surface which heats up more than another is a potential thermal generator. A dark car park, peat-covered moorland or even the land in the wind-shadow in the lee of a hill may provide a source of thermals

between 2,000 and 6,500 ft above sea level in the British Isles, and increases steadily as the day warms up, reaching a peak in mid-afternoon. Their vertical growth is limited by the temperature of the thermal which originated them dropping to that of the surrounding air.

Repeated thermals originating from one source will form a line of cumulus clouds downwind. These are known to fliers as 'cloud streets', and it is the aim of cross country pilots to connect with a cloud street and fly from thermal to thermal as indicated by the clouds. On some golden days this is achieved and dreams come true.

When the sky is covered with cumulus joined together, the result is **Stratocumulus** which rapidly becomes grey and boring, although there may still be patches of very strong lift under it. However, the pilot must be wary of strong lift beneath clouds, and be able to recognise the presence or development of **Cumulo-Nimbus** (cu-nimb). This is that enemy of aviators, the thunder cloud. Whereas the friendly cumulus puffs are limited in their vertical growth, the cu-nimb exhibits no such restraint. Moist warm air powers upwards—often aided and abetted by an advancing front—and condenses, which releases quantities of latent heat (back to school physics again). This energy then effectively continues to fuel the process and the cloud-building

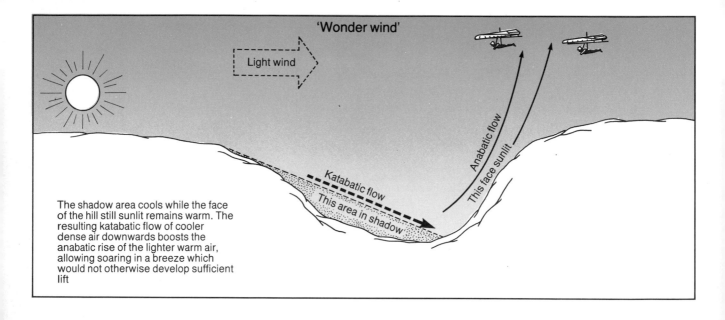

The shadow area cools while the face of the hill still sunlit remains warm. The resulting katabatic flow of cooler dense air downwards boosts the anabatic rise of the lighter warm air, allowing soaring in a breeze which would not otherwise develop sufficient lift

'Wonder wind'

Light wind

Anabatic flow

This face sunlit

Katabatic flow

This area in shadow

can roar on upwards to enormous heights. Vertical winds within the cloud can easily exceed 2,000 ft per minute, and the luckless hang glider pilot straying into a cu-nimb is unlikely to be able to brag about his experiences afterwards. Even if the turbulence doesn't get him, the frostbite or lightning will. The cu-nimb is the only cloud which can build through almost the whole depth of the usable atmosphere: the others are relatively shallow.

Altostratus and Altocumulus are the middle height clouds (approx. 10–20,000 ft) which are primarily notable for their nuisance value and the way they make the day grey.

The **Cirrus** group are the very high (20,000–40,000 ft) thin clouds of ice crystals. The presence of

stranded cirrus 'mares tails' in an otherwise blue sky often indicates an approaching cold front.

Those clouds already described may be seen anywhere over the country. The next group result from the air being forced to change its height because of ground features:

Orographic cloud is formed on a hilltop by the wind being deflected upwards over the hill. The resulting temperature drop can be enough to initiate condensation. Ridge-soaring pilots should be alive to the danger of this sort of hill fog forming around them.

A **Cap cloud** is caused in the same way, but remains stationary clear of the top of the hill. It is a close relation of the **Lenticular** or **Wave cloud** which often forms

along the apex of waves set up in the lee of mountain ranges.

The 'wonder wind' effect

Some sites are celebrated for the way they produce smooth evening ridge lift which yields height gains out of all proportion to the strength of the wind.

In heavily wooded areas such as the eastern United States, the trees on the valley floors act as great storage heaters during the day and release the heat as the sun goes down. Pilots of all levels of experience enjoy floating maybe a thousand feet above the ridge in smooth air while watching the lights

Gliders on buoyant evening air in the Pennines

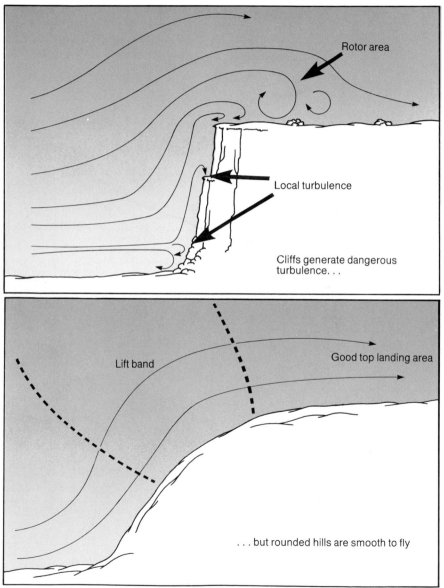

Rotor area

Local turbulence

Cliffs generate dangerous turbulence. . .

Lift band

Good top landing area

. . . but rounded hills are smooth to fly

of towns many miles distant appear in the gathering dusk. Take care not to be so beguiled by the view that you end up with the landing field in darkness.

A similar effect occurs on westerly-facing valley sides in other countries. The opposite slope will have been in the shade for a long time while the flying site remains in the sun. The air over the shaded side cools and tends to slide down the slope, in turn boosting the lift on the flying side. The downslope flow is called a **katabatic** wind, while the upward one is **anabatic**. Pilots call these evening boosts in lift either the 'Magic Lift' or 'Wonder Wind'.

Turbulence

After all this evidence that air is on the move all the time, we will look at what happens when a glider is launched into a mass of molecules of air which are hurrying on their customary way from a high pressure area to a low, by way of a convenient hill.

A good picture of how air behaves when it meets obstructions can be formed by looking at the water in a stream: you will immediately see not only how it builds up in front of a ridge, but also how it speeds up as it passes through narrow gaps. You can see how the flow actually reverses in larger eddies behind a projection from the bank, or how waves are amplified via a succession of underwater rocks. Note particularly how a smooth stone allows a smooth flow but a sharp one initiates turbulence.

All these effects have their exact counterparts in air, and the hang glider pilot must automatically visualise the flow to avoid dangerous turbulence or sinking air. There *will* be turbulence in the lee of trees, buildings or other hills: the windspeed *will* increase in a gap in the hill (venturi effect) and the flier must not be caught out by it. Constant observation and caution are vital in this sport which is so unforgiving to the pilot who does not bother to take his learning seriously.

Because your glider flies very slowly compared with other aircraft it will remain in hostile conditions longer: it lacks the speed to fly quickly away from sink in the lee of a hill or slice through turbulence on the way into a tree-surrounded landing field. Consequently, anticipation and understanding are as important as learning by personal experience. In many cases the personal experience may not allow you a second chance.

There *will* be turbulence downwind of obstructions

The Beaufort Scale

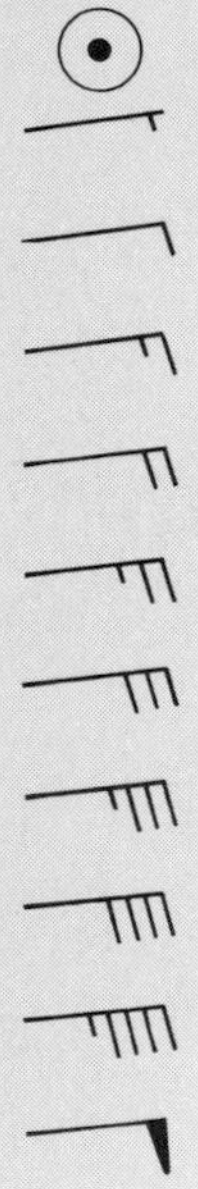

Symbol	Force	Description	Effects	Wind kt	Windsock
	0	Calm	Smoke rises vertically	1	
	1	Light air	Wind shows smoke drift; may not disturb windsock.	1 – 3	
	2	Light breeze	Wind felt on face. Leaves rustle.	4 – 6	
	3	Gentle breeze	Leaves in constant motion. Flags lift.	7 – 10	
	4	Moderate wind	Dust swirls. Small branches move.	11 – 15	
	5	Fresh wind	Small trees sway. Microlights blow over.	16 – 21	
	6	Strong wind	Large branches sway. Umbrellas uncontrollable.	22 – 27	
	7	Moderate gale	Difficulty walking against wind.	28 – 33	
	8	Gale	Twigs break off trees.	34 – 40	
	9	Strong gale	Chimney pots take off.	41 – 47	
	10	Whole gale	Trees take off.	48 – 55	

Gale warnings are issued if the wind is expected to increase to force 8 or gusts of 43 knots or more are expected. The word *imminent* means within 6 hours, *soon* means 6 – 12 hours and *later* means more than 12 hours.

Visibility

Good	More than 5 nautical miles
Moderate	2 – 5 nautical miles
Poor	900 metres – 2 nautical miles
Mist/ haze	1000 metres – 2000 metres
Fog	Less than 1000 metres at sea or 700 metres on land
Dense fog	Less than 20 metres

Fronts

warm front

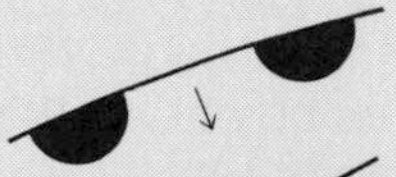

cold front

occluded

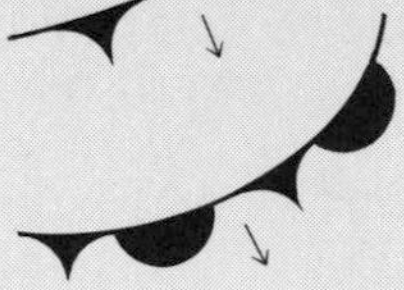

Here the surface wind is quite light, but the abundant wave-clouds are evidence of greater strength at altitude

 5. Soaring

The essential pre-flight hang check. An assistant sees that the harness is not twisted while the pilot checks his height above the bar

The pilot leaving training school is a bit like a car without an engine. The steering and brakes are adequate, but performance only lasts for a short time while going downhill.

The art of soaring lies in steering the glider into rising air and then keeping it there. Normally the first step towards learning this art is to master ridge lift.

All the time the glider is flying it is travelling down through the air at about 200 ft per minute. However, the wind encountering a hillside is deflected upwards, and it does not have to be travelling very fast for a proportion of it to move upwards considerably faster than that magical 200 ft per minute.

The area of rising air in front of a hill is called the *lift band*. It will vary in size and strength according to the size and steepness of the hill, and the strength and direction of the wind.

As a novice you will probably have flown straight out through the lift band several times on the way to your Pilot One certificate. The route to Pilot Two lies along the hill and in the lift band. Here is how to stay aloft and enjoy it: you have learned how to take off and land your glider,

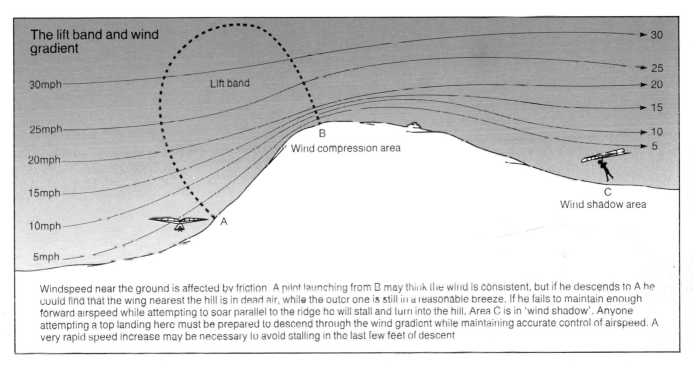

The lift band and wind gradient

30mph
25mph
20mph
15mph
10mph
5mph

Lift band

A

B
Wind compression area

C
Wind shadow area

30
25
20
15
10
5

Windspeed near the ground is affected by friction. A pilot launching from B may think the wind is consistent, but if he descends to A he could find that the wing nearest the hill is in dead air, while the outer one is still in a reasonable breeze. If he fails to maintain enough forward airspeed while attempting to soar parallel to the ridge he will stall and turn into the hill. Area C is in 'wind shadow'. Anyone attempting a top landing here must be prepared to descend through the wind gradient while maintaining accurate control of airspeed. A very rapid speed increase may be necessary to avoid stalling in the last few feet of descent

and how to make turns safely. Today you are going to ridge soar for the first time. You may be the one-in-a-thousand gifted pilot who will be able to launch, turn and fly with precision quite instinctively. It is more probable that the following routine will ease the path for you.

Firstly, check the wind. Use a meter, and be sure that the breeze is blowing square-on for these first flights. Anything between 14–20 mph should do nicely. Then have a good look at the hill. You will probably have launched from it

several times before, but there will be many factors you will not have noticed previously. Dead straight ridges exist almost exclusively on the drawing boards of motorway engineers. The ones from which we fly usually embody a series of humps and hollows and changes in direction. So take a good look. Check that you know the point at which the hill starts to curve away out of wind and be prepared to turn before there. Check if the ridge rises in the direction in which you plan to fly. If it does, you will not

seem to be climbing as fast as you really are, and you could be fooled into flying out and down when all that was really needed was a good 180° turn. Check if there are any small bowls formed in the ridge under your path—the lift is often stronger in such a bowl, and it may be a good spot to make a turn without losing height. Above all, check with experienced pilots on the hill. They will tell you if your planned flight is sensible. Ask about hazards—that little bowl you thought would be a good turning

point may actually be a celebrated local turbulence generator, and the best place to find out about that is on the ground. Do not be afraid to tell the locals that this is one of your first soaring attempts. If the club is any good, they will pass the word around and leave you more space in the air. Then check that you

remember the rules of the air. The 'break right' rule is no longer theory: you could well be using it in a minute or two.

If it is wintertime the thermal activity will probably be slight, and the air relatively smooth throughout the day. In summer, thermals may make your ridge too rough until well

A helper steadies the nose of the glider before launch

on in the afternoon. Again take advice from experienced pilots and be prepared to wait.

Assuming all is well, count the gliders in the air, decide in which direction your first turn will be, perform all your usual checks, and

launch! That first turn immediately becomes the priority. Keeping a reasonable amount of flying speed on, start to turn parallel to the hill as soon as you are comfortably clear of launch. This will not feel entirely natural, because on your flights up to now you have become used to getting quite a lot of ground clearance before making any manoeuvres. Instinct will try to tell you to get as far from the hard hillside as possible. Persevere. Make that vital first controlled turn with care and deliberation. Do not worry if you have not found the stirrup and are still 'semi-prone'. Airspeed and the turn are everything, and if you have those two elements correct you are now cruising along parallel to the hill. You will be level with, or slightly above takeoff and two or three spans out from the ridge. Now is the time to get comfortable in the harness and prepare for the next big event, the 180° turn which will bring you back along the ridge while still in the lift band. Actually the turn will have to be more than 180° otherwise each beat will be a little further from the ridge and after two or three you will be at the bottom. The turn will be more difficult than you expected, because towards the end of it you will really be flying slightly back towards the hillside, and again instinct will not want anything to do with it. Conduct this

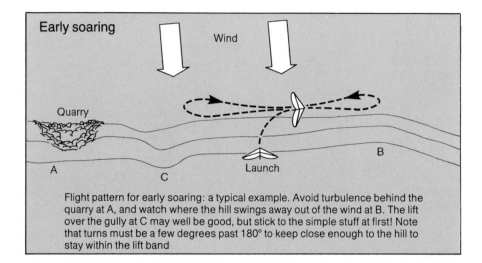

Early soaring

Wind

Quarry

A

C

Launch

B

Flight pattern for early soaring: a typical example. Avoid turbulence behind the quarry at A, and watch where the hill swings away out of the wind at B. The lift over the gully at C may well be good, but stick to the simple stuff at first! Note that turns must be a few degrees past 180° to keep close enough to the hill to stay within the lift band

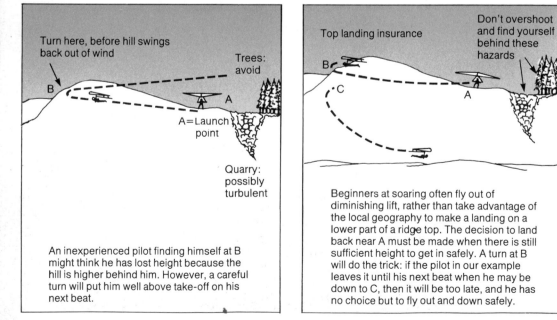

Turn here, before hill swings back out of wind

B

Trees: avoid

A

A=Launch point

Quarry: possibly turbulent

An inexperienced pilot finding himself at B might think he has lost height because the hill is higher behind him. However, a careful turn will put him well above take-off on his next beat.

Top landing insurance

Don't overshoot and find yourself behind these hazards

B

C

A

Beginners at soaring often fly out of diminishing lift, rather than take advantage of the local geography to make a landing on a lower part of a ridge top. The decision to land back near A must be made when there is still sufficient height to get in safely. A turn at B will do the trick: if the pilot in our example leaves it until his next beat when he may be down to C, then it will be too late, and he has no choice but to fly out and down safely.

An ill-judged top-landing can lead to serious
retrieve problems . . .

turn according to the textbooks, and it will make you into a soaring pilot. Plan it and fly it. Check clear around and behind Pull on a little extra speed, initiate roll, push out a little and fly the glider round until you are facing the way you came. Pull on a hint more speed while flying those few extra vital degrees past 180°, then straighten up and settle once more in the lift band. Soon you will be cruising back past takeoff feeling tense but elated. Repeat the process at the other end of your

beat and you can honestly claim to have soared. Then keep on doing it until either the wind or your concentration begins to fail. Fifteen or twenty minutes is plenty for these early flights, so fly out and down before you become overtired either mentally or physically. Top landing will come a little later.

During your soaring you may well encounter the wake turbulence generated behind another hang glider. This effect can be rather unnerving at first—particularly if it

catches you in the middle of a turn. Fortunately the turbulence is very localised, and usually you are through it before you can react. Quite soon you will be able to guess where it is likely to occur and will not be taken by surprise so often.

Soaring turns
In the early stages of soaring you will almost certainly over-control. Your progress back and forth along the ridge will be via a series of coarse changes of speed with your

50

The concealed crossboom is just visible within the double surface of this elegant glider. Keith Cockroft on a Sensor 510

Simple ridge soaring. The author in the Pennines. Note yellow parachute bridle, twistlock karabiner and white back-up suspension loop

body moving back and forth over a range of a foot (25 cm) or more. Similarly your turns will be jerky and of random radius. Smoothness only comes with practice, but if from early on you try to fly smoothly and economically then your overall progress will certainly be more rapid.

When you are soaring in reliable lift conditions, set yourself simple tasks to perform, such as turning precisely over a certain point on the ground. Then concentrate on being in exactly the correct direction when coming out of a turn and back into level flight, so that no reverse correction is needed.

See how most gliders make a gentle flat turn when the pilot simply moves his legs a little to one side.

Competition pilots working for lift beneath developing cumulus. The rule about circling in the same direction does not seem to be particularly closely observed in this case!

This is the start of a yawing turn, a technique which may be useful later on when trying to get centred in weak, ill-defined thermals.

Then as confidence grows, try entering tighter turns using a quite defined 'speed-up'/input roll/push out/centre on bar/roll out sequence. Naturally, all these turns must be made in the direction *away* from the ridge.

On paper this all sounds quite logical and straightforward, but on the hill there will be other fliers present. Regardless of all other considerations, you must keep a constant lookout and fly defensively. It is your absolute responsibility to know where all the other gliders are, and to know who has priority in all circumstances. Vigilance is vital, not an optional extra.

As your turns become more ambitious, two things will almost certainly happen. Firstly you will be tempted to try a 360° circle, and secondly you will get your speed wrong in a turn and enter your first sideslip. It is much better if you encounter the sideslip before you try a 360°, rather than during it.

The sideslip occurs because you have too great an angle of bank relative to speed. The correct reaction is to pull on speed rapidly before weight shifting to the 'uphill' side of the control bar. You will lose quite a lot of height during this manoeuvre, and so it is essential that you are at a really safe height forward of the ridge.

360° turns are not really very difficult, provided you can fly good accurate 180°s and manage varying angles of bank competently. It is, however, very difficult to say when the time is right to attempt your first one—so much depends on the amount of height available on the day, how turbulent the air, how crowded the site, and how prepared you feel. The shape and size of the hill also has a lot to do with it: flying well out from a mountain and performing a nil wind 360° on the way to a bottom landing may be a good idea. A similar exercise on a 300 ft (100 m) ridge with a strong wind blowing would be suicidal!

Do not be shy about asking an experienced pilot on the hill—a BHGA Observer would be ideal—if it is a good occasion to try 360°s for the first time.

Top landing

While Britain lacks spectacular high mountain sites, there is great compensation in the fact that many of our hills are top-landable, unlike the rugged Alps or tree covered hills of the eastern USA.

Once the simple theory is understood, the practice of landing back on top of a suitable hill is easier than anywhere else. Put simply, you fly your glider back over the edge of the ridge and into air which is no longer rising faster than your aircraft sinks.

The first priority is to be sure that the air will be smooth all the way to your landing. Remember that it will flow over the ground in much the same way as it flows over your wing: it follows smooth curves faithfully, but resents being asked to change direction rapidly. Therefore over a round hillside the transition from the vertical flow in the lift band to the horizontal one over the top of the site will be progressive and safe to fly through. At the lip of a cliff things are very different. The flow breaks up radically, and turbulent 'rotors' can form which are extremely dangerous. Study the hill in the same way that you did before attempting to soar, and decide where you will land and what will be the safest approach line. Again, check with the regular fliers who will know the tricky spots better than you.

Top landing approaches

1 Crosswind tracking
This is the approach you should use for all your early top landings. You must be able to sustain at least a

Alone in the sky above the North Yorkshire Moors

Top landing activity at a busy site

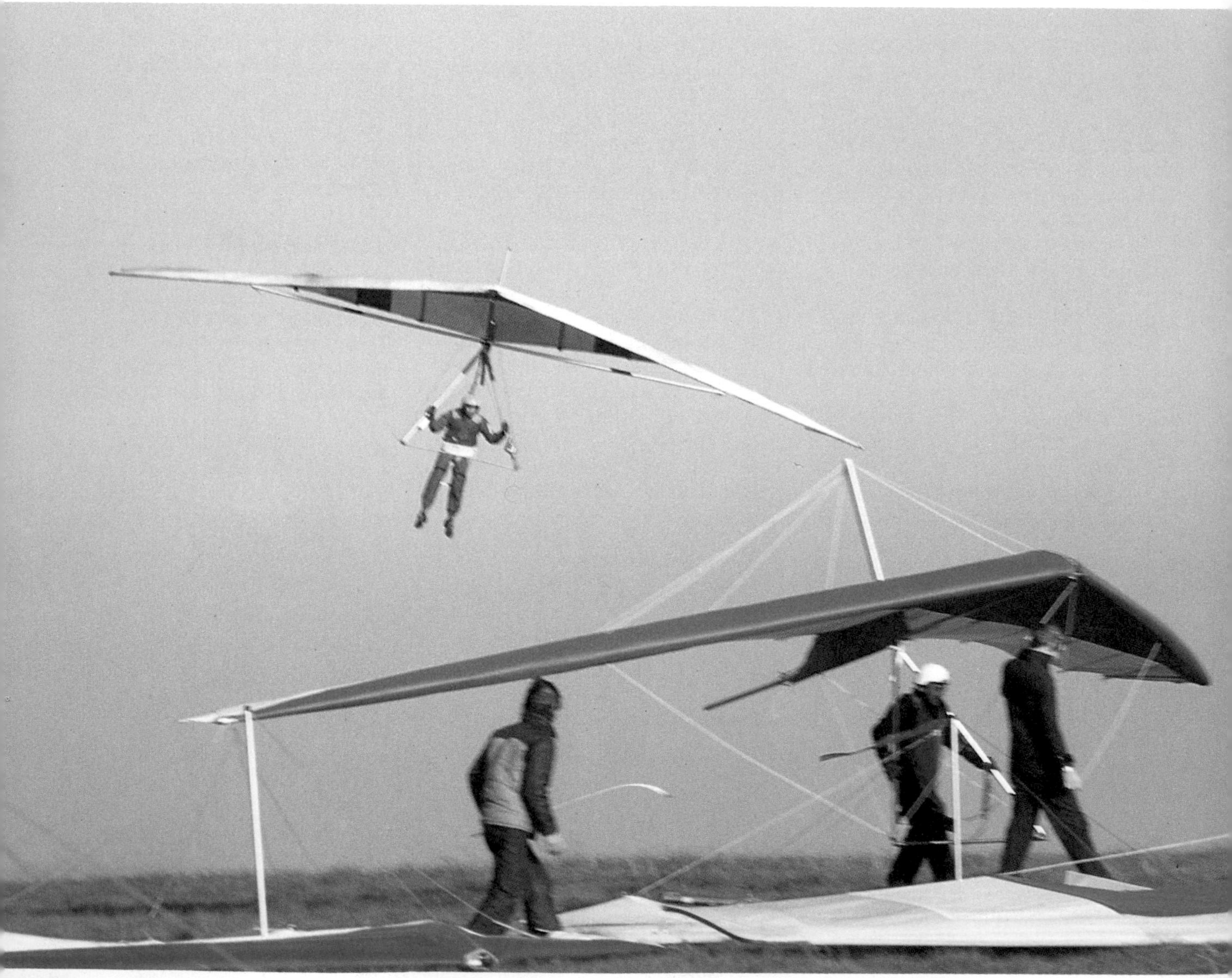

The pilot, Peter Anstey, is fully out of prone for a nicely relaxed top landing approach. Glider: UP Comet

hundred feet over the ridge, and preferably rather more, before attempting the landing. Let us assume you are soaring quite confidently and feel that now is the time to get in on top. Spend another couple of beats planning your approach. Use all the evidence you have to determine whether or not the wind is square on to the ridge. If it is not—and it rarely is—your approach should be from the direction which is slightly into the wind. Check not only that the actual area in which you plan to touch down is clear and suitable, but also that your flight track will not take you over any cliffs, quarries or trees which may be turbulence generators. Once quite satisfied, decide the point on the ridge where your approach will start, and when there, allow your glider to fly a few degrees back over the edge and aim for a spot in the sky a small distance behind where you intend to land. When at that point, be quite positive in squaring up the glider directly into wind again, come out of the prone position and fly down. Note we say fly down. You will be passing through a wind gradient and speed adjustment and control are vital all the way to the ground. Beware of the dreaded 'dead air' close to the ground and be

A careless top landing can result in a blow-over

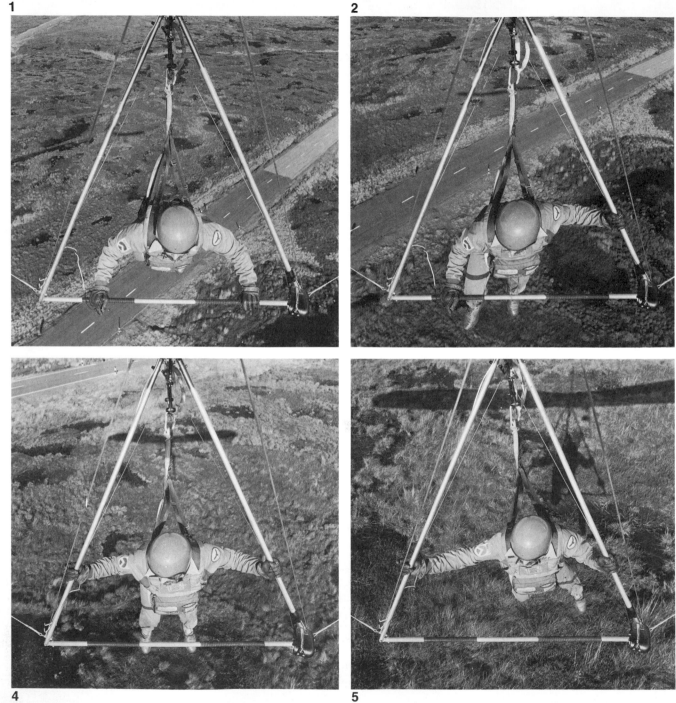

3

6

A typical top landing:

(1) Approach: keeping a little speed on, the body is rotated upright

(2) Feet down, grip is transferred to the uprights

(3) Weightshifting through turbulent air. Note glider shadow on road

(4) Level again and square into wind

(5) Almost down, but quite a lot of last-minute weightshift is needed

(6) Safe landing at walking speed

High bank plus some push-out results in a tight turn

Opposite weightshift is used here to compensate for poor initial co-ordination into turn

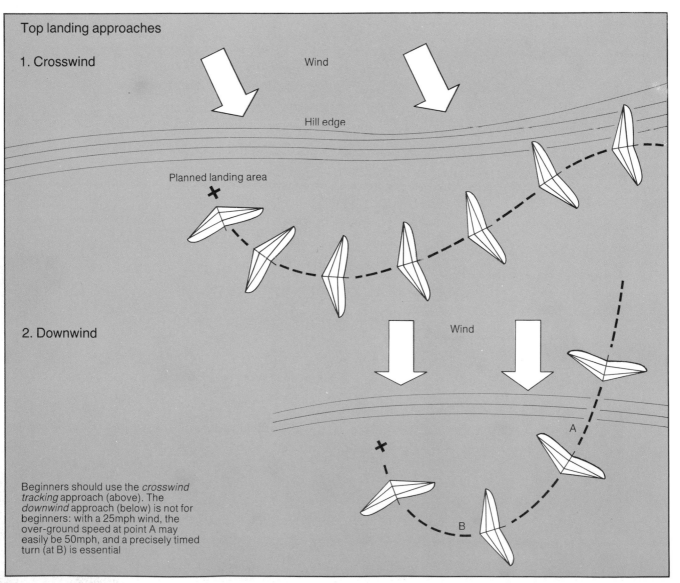

Top landing approaches

1. Crosswind

Wind

Hill edge

Planned landing area

2. Downwind

Wind

A

B

Beginners should use the *crosswind tracking* approach (above). The *downwind* approach (below) is not for beginners: with a 25mph wind, the over-ground speed at point A may easily be 50mph, and a precisely timed turn (at B) is essential

prepared to pull on lots of speed to avoid a stall. Just as big a hazard may be flaring out in the same way that you always have previously when bottom landing. If there is much strength in the wind you may well be blown over backwards!

2 Downwind approach
Not for beginners. This involves flying directly downwind over the edge of the hill and then making a precise and rapid 180° turn before landing. Bearing in mind that groundspeed may be over 50 mph (80 kph) on the downwind leg, the need for precision and confidence become obvious. Repeat, not for beginners.

3 Rearward drift
This used to be quite common, and indeed many first top landings on earlier gliders were executed via this style and were quite involuntary. The pilot would find himself unable to penetrate out from the hill in a strong wind: relaxing the bar a little allowed him to drift back into air which was no longer rising, and down he would gradually come. The technique is only possible in strongish winds and is not to be encouraged as it is sloppy and potentially hazardous.

Top landing tips
Always think airspeed. Sometimes it will feel as if the ground is flashing

Mountain soaring in Japan

past underneath at an alarming rate. Do not worry about that: concentrate on airspeed and avoid pushing the bar out to slow up when travelling downwind.

After you have come out of prone try and relax a little: if your body is over-tense you will tend to over-control and the descent will be a perpetual battle. Just keep an eye on the ground below to ensure that you are not drifting off wind, and use small control inputs until you have landed safely. As soon as you are on the ground, step through the control frame and hold onto the front wires while you check your position and the strength of the wind. Many a top landing has turned into an accident because the pilot relaxed the second his toes touched the grass!

On your first few top landings, do not become disheartened if they are some distance from the spot you had in mind. Concentrate on making a safe landing rather than anything else. Accuracy will come with time.

Never come in close behind or over parked gliders. Sooner or later you will misjudge things a little, and sail repairs are costly in both cash and friends.

Do not be afraid of overshooting. If you are too near the front of the hill to get down safely, then admit it early on, get back into prone, and fly out and go round again. We all do it

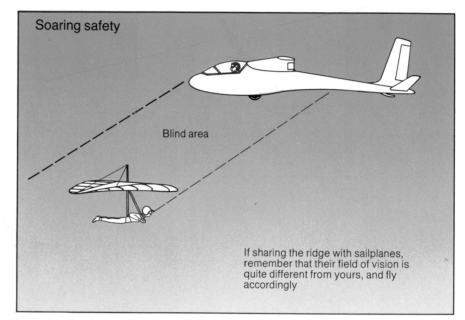

Soaring safety

Blind area

If sharing the ridge with sailplanes, remember that their field of vision is quite different from yours, and fly accordingly

from time to time and it is nothing to be ashamed of.

When launching from a site which is being top-landed always check behind as well as above and to the sides—someone may be overshooting just as you are about to set off. Remember—you can hold back, but he cannot!

Thermal soaring

After you have acquired some flying time in the lift band, you will notice that you sometimes enter turbulence which is unrelated to ground features. Unexpected lift or sink will also be associated with this

turbulence, and at first you will find this rather off-putting. The most probable explanation is that you are encountering your first thermals.

At this stage in your flying career it is simplest to think of thermals as short-lived columns of air which are rising more rapidly than the rest because they are warmer. Their strength and size will vary tremendously, but if you can stay in the middle of one you will be able to gain much more height than is possible using ridge lift only. It is very difficult to form a mental image of a thermal, but the feel of your glider as you fly along your ridge will provide many clues.

A lone flier makes the most of evening lift in the Pennines. Some wave cloud is evident, while orographic mist forms over distant Pendle Hill

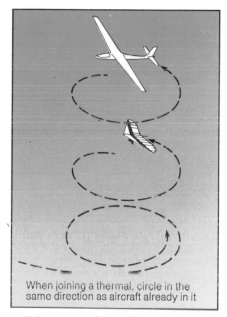

When joining a thermal, circle in the same direction as aircraft already in it

If the nose of the glider feels as if it is being tugged upwards but the plane does not attempt to roll, then you have flown straight into the side of a thermal. If you keep going straight along the ridge you can expect to lose height as you exit from the other side. If your thermal was a strong one, you may find yourself being quite violently tipped forward as you leave—an experience often graphically described as 'going over the falls'. The time between entry and exit can give some indication of the size of the thermal through which you have just flown.

Similarly, strong lift under one

wing will occur if just half of your glider enters the thermal, and the correct reaction is to weight-shift towards the lifting wing. Naturally if this happens when you are very close to the hill and flying too slowly, you may find yourself being rolled into the ground. This is one reason why it is always vital to fly well above stalling speed when close to the ridge so that you have instant control response.

Once you have become accustomed to the changes in vertical speed which accompany thermal activity, and are able to turn competently while remaining aware of the position of other gliders on the ridge, it is time to start learning to climb up with the thermals.

Next time you are well above the ridge and you experience that characteristic upward surge via the control bar, keep going for a second or two and then, if all is clear, perform a 180° turn to face the way you have come. With any luck the whole turn will take place within the thermal and you may be aware that you have climbed above gliders you saw above you on your previous beat. Now try another turn and ease the bar out as far as feels safe. If the thermal is a decent one you will ascend in it via a series of 'S' turns, but beware of being carried back behind the ridge.

Repeated attempts at 'S' turning in thermals will teach you a lot about the nature of this form of lift, from which it is but a short step to circling in it via a series of 360° turns.

Once you have gained some proficiency at keeping your 360°s within the thermal, then it is time to think about investing in a variometer: you are on the threshold of advanced flying.

Many more hours of pleasant and confidence-building ridge flying will be necessary before venturing off cross-country like the pilot in Chapter 7, but that will surely come with time.

Wave soaring

This is a variation on ridge lift; the difference is that the height gains can be truly amazing, and although the presence of wave is often predictable, one cannot be guaranteed to connect with it.

The existence of the wave depends on a number of conditions: there must be a hill or range of hills a distance upwind of your flying site; there must be an element of stability in the air; and the wind must be of such a speed that a wave forms which is 'in phase' with your hill.

Your first encounter with wave lift is likely to be during the evening at one of Britain's westerly-facing sites in the lee of the Pennines. After the thermals have died down you will find the ridge smooth to soar, then while cruising at say 300–400 ft above takeoff, you will feel a roughness which may be rather unnerving. If you persevere into the roughness while flying your glider at minimum sink speed you will probably climb up through it and discover that after a couple of hundred feet more height-gain the air becomes glassy-smooth. If you have instruments they will insist you are still climbing at anything between 50 and 400 ft per minute. This can continue up to amazing heights. In Britain hang gliders have reached to around the 10,000 ft mark, while the higher speed of sailplanes allows them to hold station in much stronger waves where 30,000 ft is not uncommon. If the prospect of all this ultra-smooth lift is attractive, then you should also be aware of the problems: all that free energy going upwards is surrounded by lots more going just as rapidly downwards. The rotor turbulence behind a wave can be catastrophically destructive. Bearing in mind the state of the art of hang glider design at the time of writing, beware of venturing into wave lift beyond the point where you can still fly forward.

A side effect is also that you will probably never have been anything like as high before. Do not be surprised if the sensation is unnerving—it really is not remarkable that once you have lost

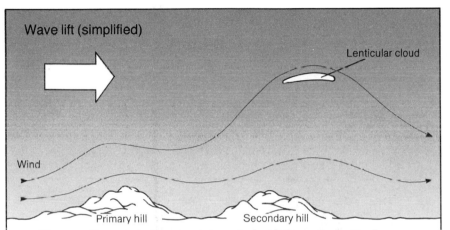

Wave lift (simplified)

Wind

Lenticular cloud

Primary hill   Secondary hill

When conditions of windspeed and atmospheric stability are favourable, the initial wave formed over the primary hill can be amplified by another ridge downwind. The vertical flow is then boosted to provide abnormally good height gains. A change in windspeed can result in the system going 'out of phase', however, and the wave may disappear rapidly. Severe turbulence downwind of the wave must always be anticipated.

Unlike most clouds, which constantly travel downwind, the lenticular cloud remains stationary, marking the apex of the wave. This is because it is constantly being formed at the front and dissipated at the rear: the wave air passes up into a temperature level at which the water vapour within it condenses, and then the water droplets evaporate as the air flows down again.

Such waves also frequently occur without the presence of a lenticular cloud, however; so it is not an infallible indicator

contact with all your familiar points of reference you feel strangely insecure. BHGA President Ann Welch advocates gradually gaining height experience, a few hundred feet at a time according to how confident you feel, and that is sound counsel indeed. However, if you allow yourself to be beguiled by the smoothness and ease of ascent provided by some waves and then suddenly appreciate that there is half a mile or more of daylight between your eyeballs and the ground, do not be surprised if you begin to feel very insecure indeed.

You will probably convince yourself that your glider has suddenly become unstable, as if it would tip over in any direction if you move at all. Your fingers will be trying to crush the control bar with a white-knuckled death-grip, and you would very much like to be down at 400 ft again! There is no instant cure, but try a few slow controlled breaths—not too much, this is no time to hyperventilate. Then if the wind is not too strong, fly a few 360°s, some to the left and some to the right, so that you reassure yourself that it is you who is really in control of the glider and not the other way about. Then concentrate on flying out forward from the hill, which will usually lead you by degrees safely out of the wave.

Often the apex of the wave is marked in the sky by a characteristic line-cloud, called a 'lenticular' because of its lens-shaped section. The formation of wave and the way it may shift in and out of phase with any particular hill is rather complex and beyond the scope of this book. It is well documented in meteorological and gliding literature.

Soaring safely

Always be aware of other gliders on the hill, and keep a constant lookout. Make all turns away from the hill when in pure ridge lift. Do plan the direction of your first turn—do not launch and then see which feels easiest. Monitor the wind direction all the time by judging your speed along the ridge, so that your top-landing approach will be into the wind. Do not attempt your first ridge soaring in thermic conditions—wait until early evening.

Coastal soaring on the Isle of Wight

Special notes on coastal soaring

Sea cliffs are very good places to soar. The air meeting the shoreline will have travelled for many miles over the relatively flat sea and so will be very smooth. Provided the nature of rotor turbulence around cliffs is understood you can enjoy many hours of airtime shared with the seagulls. However, although the air is pleasant to fly in, it cannot be too highly stressed that the sea below is quite lethal to land in. Never ever gamble on staying up on a cliff from which you cannot reach a bottom landing. Do not use a screw-locked karabiner as you will not be able to get free of the glider quickly in the event of a water landing. Consider seriously the use of buoyancy aids for both you and your glider. Remember that on a vertical cliff the amount of lift available may alter radically with only a few degrees of wind-direction change.

Beach landings can be hazardous, but the roughest of dry land is safer than even quite shallow water. Glider: Airwave 'Magic I'

If you do judge everything wrongly and find yourself going down, land among rocks rather than even quite shallow water. Bruising is better than drowning, and drowning is a very real possibility in as little as four or five feet of water. The amount of force which quite small waves can exert on the area of a wing is astonishing, so you must get clear of the glider at the earliest opportunity, before it either sinks or breaks up around you. If you can get rid of your gloves before splashdown, so much the better: then land as slowly as possible and GET UNCLIPPED AND CLEAR at once. Do not attempt to save your glider before you yourself are safe and have assistance. The most expensive aircraft in the world is useless if your lungs are full of water. I cannot overemphasise the danger: water landing is possibly the single most easily identified yet most simply avoided killer of hang glider pilots.

The Pilot Two Certificate

The next stage for a soaring pilot is achieving the Pilot 2 rating. This is a worthwhile qualification which demonstrates that you are truly a competent flier. Some clubs require visiting fliers to hold P2 ratings before flying certain sites, and in Germany you may be asked for your rating card before being allowed to take a glider onto the cable car to mountain takeoff points.

Pilot 2 requirements

Before applying for a pilot 2 rating the pilot must have held a Pilot 1 rating for at least four months.
The pilot must safely demonstrate:
1 30 flights, of at least 10 minutes duration; each flight must be separately logged.
2 5 flights, from each of five different sites, of which at least three are inland.
3 10 five-minute flights; 5 from each of two different sites.
4 2 stand-up top landings on each of three different sites, 2 of which must be inland.
5 3 stand-up landings, within a 12 metres (40 ft) diameter area, after flights of at least one minute's duration. These landings may be top landings.
6 3 nil-wind takeoffs, ending in stand-up landings.

7 the flying of the FAI Delta Bronze tasks. These are:
A distance of not less than 2 km must be flown over a course of not less than 0.5 km between 2 turn points. A controlled landing must be made within 25 metres of a designated spot.
A short field landing, within 40 metres of a 5 metre high obstruction, followed by a controlled stand-up landing. Five flights of not less than 5 minutes' duration, and five landings within 25 metres of a spot. (This requirement will have been done at an early stage of Pilot 2 task 1, provided that the landing complied).
8 Precise 180° turns, both gently and steeply banked, to the left and right.

Discuss and safely demonstrate:—
9   a. good control in turns
     b. stall recovery from straight and level flight into wind.
     c. recognition of the onset of a stall and its prevention in a positive manner.
     d. how to cope with wind gradient and the importance of air speed on a landing approach.
     e. the crosswind tracking top landing method.

Discuss and show thorough understanding of:—
10   a. the BHGA Code of Good Practice, Flying Rules and Recommendations.
      b. glide angle control.
      c. Spin, Yaw and Slideslip recovery.
      d. the three top landing approach methods, (crosswind tracking, downwind, glide angle control, with strong winds), and their associated advantages and dangers in certain conditions.
      e. the stall in turns, its recognition, prevention and recovery and its implications in turns near the ground.
      f. the effects of wind gradient and gusts in both upwind and downwind flight.
      g. the effects of upwind terrain features and the flow of air over obstructions.
      h. different flying characteristics and pilot requirements of the hang gliders within his club.
      i. how he would cope with difficult weather conditions on his club sites.

Pass BHGA Examination
11 on Air Law, Navigation and Meteorology applicable to the flying of hang gliders, particularly on cross-country flights, within a pilot's 'local' area.

After becoming P2 rated, a pilot

may apply to his club to become a BHGA Observer. If his club's committee consider that he has the maturity of outlook, integrity and genuine willingness to help developing pilots improve their standard, his application will be endorsed to the BHGA. The Observer badge carries no prestige or status but simply shows that the holder is prepared to witness the tasks involved in the Pilot Rating Scheme, and offer advice on them when appropriate. The detailed requirements for Pilot 2 and Pilot 3 are likely to change in 1985, but the overall flying standard will be unaltered.

Len Hull's Magic III is very fully equipped: a Skymaster parachute is mounted on the keel, and a small drogue 'chute to steepen glide during landing approach is visible on the right-hand upright. The vario incorporates a fan-driven a.s.i. The bent bottom bar is an option which gives more comfort in flight and permits extra speed to be pulled on when in the vertical position

6. Advanced equipment

Instruments

Once the technique of sustaining flight in ridge lift has been mastered, it is time to think about investing in instruments. The basics are an altimeter and a variometer, and the choice of suitable examples can have a great effect on the quality of a pilot's flying.

The altimeter
This is really only a variant on the barometer, with a scale reading in feet or metres rather than millibars. By measuring the drop in air pressure as one ascends, it indicates height. The pressure changes to be registered are small, so the altimeter is of necessity a precision instrument, and one worth having is unlikely to be cheap.

Many pilots prefer the Swiss-made Thommen instrument which was originally developed for mountaineers. With a sweep of only 3,000 ft per revolution of the pointer, and a temperature-compensated movement, it is well suited to British conditions. It will detect height differences of as little as 25 ft (8 m).

Ex-RAF altimeters are also widely used, although their relative bulk and fragility mean that they are not quite ideal for our sport.

Parachutists' instruments such as the Diplex work well, but a sweep of 8,000 ft per revolution increases the minimum effective height change which can be read to about 100 ft.

At the time of writing, a number of electronic altimeters are coming on to the market. Early examples have proved somewhat temperamental in damp conditions, but these

The Diplex altimeter

Variometer, altimeter, compass and a.s.i.

instruments, battery powered and metering from a pressure sensitive cell, will certainly become increasingly popular.

The main features to check when buying an altimeter are that it is easy to zero, and that service and spares are available.

Variometers (varios)
Varios are one of the oldest aeronautical instruments; crude examples were used by balloon pilots 150 years ago. Constant development by sailplane fliers since the 1930s has led to a highly sophisticated range now being available.

The vario measures the *rate* of climb or descent at any moment, and is invaluable for making the most of thermal lift.

The simplest versions work by taking advantage of the fact that air in a flask will want to remain at the same pressure as that outside. If the flask has a single orifice, the air will flow out through it as the flask moves up into thinner air, and back in when it comes down into denser air. By arranging for the air on its way into or out of the flask to move polystyrene pellets up transparent tubes, a visible indication of climb or sink is available.

The most commonly used pellet variometer in hang gliding is the Makkiki, a simple and small unit.

Of course, the pellet vario is

The Colver was one of the first electronic varios to become popular, and it is still favoured by many experts because of its high-volume flask which gives very good response

lift without having his eyes glued to a dial all the time. The benefit for a hang glider flier is obvious, and a variety of chirps, bleeps and whines from the varios can be heard whenever a gaggle of aircraft are together on a ridge. In fact, the cheapest instruments do not even have a dial, but rely exclusively on a tone.

Most varios in current use work on the same principle as the pellet variety, but rather than lifting pellets, the air moving in and out of the flask cools one of a pair of heat-sensing elements, called thermistors, more than the other. The electrical resistance of a thermistor varies according to its temperature, and the resulting current change appears on a meter as an indication of lift or sink according to which way the air is flowing, and how fast.

Further up the price range are electronic varios working from a small pressure transducer. The American-made Ball unit is typical of this variety, which is likely to become more popular as the cost of the pressure cells becomes increasingly competitive.

All the electronic instruments are sensitive and effective. The thermistor types usually need to be switched on a few minutes before takeoff in order to stabilise and be zeroed correctly. They will also tolerate less rough handling than

the transducer variety.

The varios described so far are simple instruments well suited to the slow-flying hang gliders in use up until the last year or so. They only indicate that the aircraft is going up or down, and take no account of why. You will know that if you are soaring at maximum glide speed along a ridge and then rapidly slow down to min sink, you will gain altitude as you slow down. A simple vario will show this climb in exactly the same way that it would if the height gain originated from thermal lift. Sailplane pilots call such pilot-induced climbs 'stick thermals'. The latest generation of

The Ball 651 combined variometer and digital altimeter

purely visual, as is the Thommen aneroid vario which is a very compact dial instrument. Both these types have the advantage of not needing batteries to power them.

Electronic varios score because it is simple to arrange for an audible tone to work in conjunction with the meter, so the pilot can 'hear' sink or

As the instrument moves up into less dense atmosphere, higher-pressure air in the flask expands and flows out, moving the 'up' pellet up its tapered transparent tube while the 'down' pellet is seated at the base of its tube. When moving down into denser air the whole process is reversed

The Thunderbird vario incorporates an airspeed sensor which makes it one of the first 'total energy' instruments to be made for hang gliding

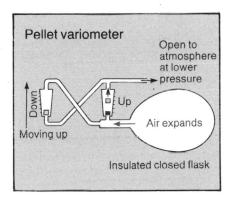

Pellet variometer

Open to atmosphere at lower pressure

Up

Down

Air expands

Moving up

Insulated closed flask

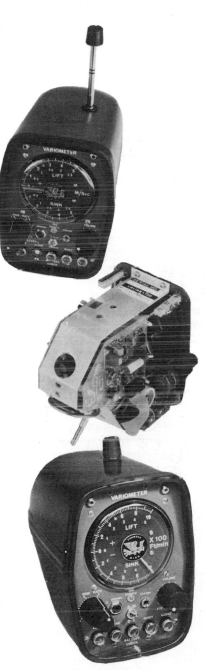

varios overcomes this effect by incorporating a compensating device which adjusts the response of the instrument via a speed-sensitive probe connected to it. These are called 'total energy variometers', and are now normal in sailplanes. Bearing in mind that hang gliders are relatively slow, and that it is also rather difficult to choose a place on the glider to mount the sensing probe where the airflow is sufficiently undisturbed at all angles of attack, it is questionable whether total energy varios are of practical benefit to any but the most advanced cross-country flier at this time.

Another new development is the 'MacCready Ring' or 'speed to fly ring'. This is a tool for the very advanced soaring pilot, in the form of an extra scale calibrated in mph, which fits around the outside of the

vario scale. Thus the vario needle will not only indicate so many feet per minute up or down, but will also show a flying speed. The calibration of the ring depends upon accurate information of the glider's sink rate and glide angles being available, plus a consistent airspeed indicator being fitted. If all these criteria are met, then the pilot who flies at the speed indicated should maximise the available lift and also fly most economically through sink.

The pilot about to invest in his first vario should avoid such complexities. A good simple unit with a clear read-out is all that is required. 'Try before you buy' is a good motto here. Check that it is easy to zero, and most important, returns to the same zero after you have flown with it for an hour or so. Check that the tone is not offensive and can be adjusted or switched to 'up only' if required. If the unit has a spare battery and changeover switch, then so much the better. One of the laws of the air seems to be that battery failure only occurs halfway through a good cross-country flight.

Novices usually 'test' a vario by rapidly raising it from floor level to arms' stretch. This will demonstrate little beyond the fact that all models have some lag. It is the response to slow but steady climb or sink that is important. A better test is to take it for a walk up and down a flight of

Close-up of the Thunderbird with speed-sensing probe retracted

stairs and check for response and consistency of reading.

Airspeed indicators (ASI)

Because the hang glider pilot is in total contact with the element in which he flies, uninsulated by cockpit or windscreen, undisturbed by engine noise or propellor wash, an instrument to indicate speed is less important than in other fields of aviation. Indeed, any hang glider pilot who relied on a dial to avoid stalling would be asking for trouble—flying at a safe speed by sense alone is an essential acquired skill in the sport.

However, ASIs do have their uses, and various types are available. Simplest and most popular are the Ventimeter and Hall types, which operate via direct air pressure moving a disc up a graduated transparent tube. Both are quite inexpensive, but are extremely sensitive to wind direction: if not fitted to the glider at exactly the same angle for each flight, the results will be inconsistent.

Originally designed as hand-held wind meters for ground use, these gauges are normally fitted to the control frame, as they must be readily visible to the pilot. Such positioning means that the speed they record will not be the true airspeed due to the influence of the nearby wing. However, provided

Using a 'Ventimeter' to check wind speed. It must be held at the correct angle to the wind if the reading is to be accurate

the error is consistent they still have their uses.

Position error also affects the more sophisticated 'vacuum gauge' type instruments such as the Winter. This works from the depression generated in a venturi placed in the airstream. The faster the airspeed, the greater the depression. As the venturi can be installed remote from the dial, e.g. atop the kingpost, there is more likelihood of such an ASI being accurate.

Barographs

Successful claims for national and international records must be substantiated by a barograph trace. The barograph is basically an

The Replogle barograph: essential equipment for would-be record breakers

74

Jenny Ganderton checking her barograph prior to a record attempt in the challenging Owens Valley on the California/Nevada border

Below: Testing a hang-glider parachute

altimeter, the needle of which makes a line on graph paper which is mounted on a slowly-revolving drum. The drum is clockwork-powered and normally has a duration of about eight hours. Until recently the trace was made with a stylus on a sooted metal surface, but fortunately this medium has been superseded by pressure-sensitive paper.

Due to considerations of both cost and convenience, barographs are not commonly carried on hang gliders except by the most dedicated cross-country or record fliers. On many occasions the difference between an 'official' and 'unofficial' record has been the existence of a barograph trace, even though hang gliding enthusiasts themselves have never doubted the authenticity of the longer 'unofficial' record.

Parachutes

An emergency parachute is now a normal piece of equipment for the serious flier. Systems on the market are well-proven and have saved many lives. There are two basic types, harness-mounted and glider-mounted. The former is the most popular at present.

Before describing examples of each type, let us bear in mind that the demands likely to be made on a parachute suitable for a hang glider pilot are not the same as those for

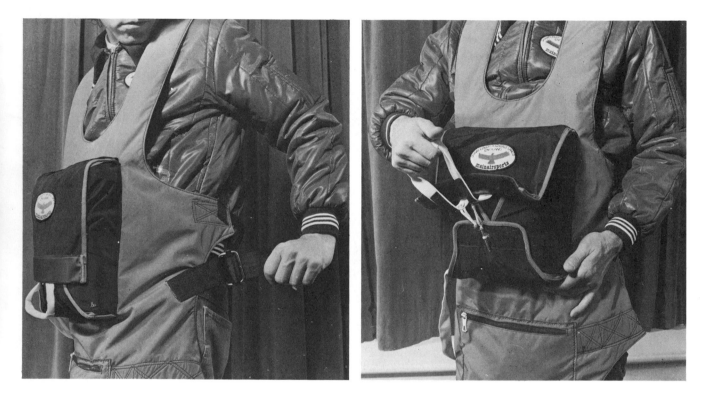

any other type of aviator. Our parachutes are expected to lower both pilot and glider together, and must deploy rapidly at a low speed. They must be capable of being thrown clear of glider debris close to the pilot, and must not be so heavy or inconvenient that fliers will be deterred from carrying them. By no means least, they must stay in their containers until activated deliberately, in spite of being roughly treated with all the other

tackle in the pilot's car!

The harness-mounted chute

As with so much hang gliding equipment this is yet another example of deceptively simple design which works well. Incorporated into the harness front is a rectangular fabric compartment held closed with Velcro. Protruding from this will be a substantial loop or handle which is attached to a nylon parcel containing the canopy and

rigging lines of the parachute. When the handle is pulled the compartment opens, leaving the pilot holding the parachute parcel which is attached to the top of his harness via about 20 ft (7 m) of 2,500 lb breaking strain tape. This parcel is then thrown away from the disabled glider into as clear a space as possible: when the bridle tape goes taut, an elastic band snaps off allowing the parcel to open and the canopy to deploy well clear of the

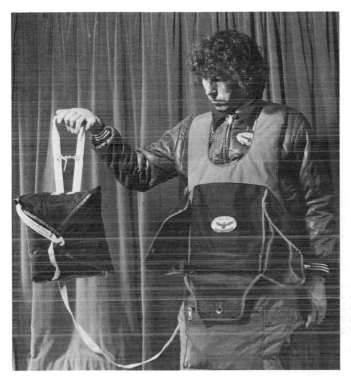

A typical harness-mounted parachute system. The outer container is sewn to the front of the harness. A backstrap provides extra security and comfort (far left). Pulling the handle opens the velcro closure and then extracts the locking pin (centre). The canopy and rigging lines remain within the deployment bag which is thrown clear of the glider. This bag does not open until the long bridle is fully extended, so the parachute should inflate only when well clear of the aircraft

glider. Glider and pilot are then lowered to the ground together.

Glider-mounted chute

Here a rigid cylindrical container is fitted to the rear keel of the glider. A long ripcord goes along the keel and down to the control frame. In certain models it may even be led down to the pilot's harness. The canopy is packed into the container behind a spring-loaded drogue chute. Pulling the ripcord handle withdraws a pin on the container lid, which flies off, closely followed by the drogue chute which promptly inflates and deploys the main canopy.

Parachute problems

Parachutes are commonly referred to as back-up systems, and should be looked upon as exactly that. They are a form of insurance for use in dire emergency, not a licence for reckless flying. The most likely reasons to use one may be as a result of airframe failure through radical turbulence, glider neglect, or mid-air collision. In all these cases pilot and glider will remain clipped together. Another, mercifully rare, disaster which can befall us is karabiner failure. To combat this the less fatalistic among us make sure that there is a second karabiner or screwed D-ring uniting the parachute bridle with the harness. A waist belt or back strap is also

Walter Schonauer resorts to unorthodox methods to keep the end of his harness out of the way during launch. Glider: 'Firebird'

Big ramp styles in Germany. Gliders: Sensor S10 and Azur

A well committed takeoff with the enclosed type of harness. Glider: Airwave 'Nimrod'

. . . and landing in a similar harness. Leg doors are open. Pilot: Tim Taft

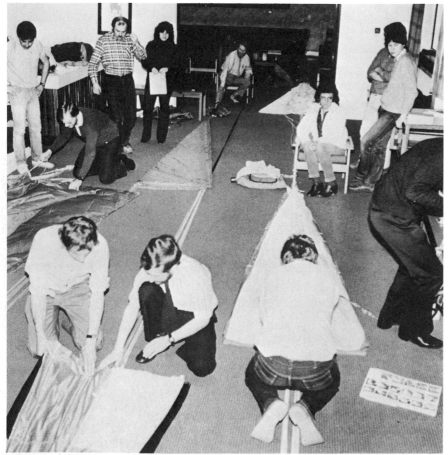

A parachute packing session at the Dales Hang Gliding Club. All canopies should be inspected and re-packed at least twice a year

necessary to ensure that the pilot is not ejected from a loose-fitting harness in the event of rapid chute deployment.

No parachute will save you from every situation, but you can improve the odds by caring for your system. Repacking is vital, and should be done at least twice a year. No attempt will be made here to describe the job as details differ between one system and another, and *you* must know that *yours* is absolutely correctly done according to the current instructions of the manufacturer. The job is by no means as daunting as some pilots imagine, and clubs can help by organising packing evenings a couple of times a season.

Include your parachute container in your pre-flight inspection routine: check that it is properly closed but clear to open when necessary. Above all, check that it is not able to burst open when you arch your body into the harness. And make sure that the opening handle is clear of the bottom bar when you are pulling on full speed. More than one pilot has happily launched from a hill only to experience the sensation of the grasp of the Almighty dragging him back to earth as his chute makes an involuntary deployment.

Similar care is essential with the keel-mounted systems. The long ripcord means that there is scope for both jamming and snagging, and so pre-flight inspections are extra important.

And do remember, all parachutes hate sunlight, heat and rain, so store them as if your life depends upon it. It does.

Harnesses
Your first harness after leaving training school will probably be an orthodox prone stirrup type. If used with an ankle loop which makes it easy to find the stirrup directly after launch, the newer pilot will have no difficulty flying fully prone.

Ballast, in the form of fine dry sand, is being added to a competition pilot's harness. Increasing the wing-loading in this way makes the glider fly faster at any given bar-position. The ballast may be released before touch-down so that the landing speed remains low

The cocoon harness can be more comfortable, and certainly offers more warmth for winter flying. Also with a faired-in parachute container the drag should be slightly reduced. Disadvantages are additional bulk to carry up hills, plus rather more awkwardness at takeoff; the bottom portion of the harness has to be held out of the way of the pilot's running legs.

The Bullet or Supp types of enclosed harness are a later attempt at streamlining the pilot by enclosing his entire body except for head and arms. The flier is contained in a flexible chrysalis-like suit with a suspension point in the middle of the back and a pair of 'bomb-doors' through which to lower his legs. These harnesses are really comfortable, although very bulky to carry. Takeoff is no problem as the 'tail' portion is behind the pilot's legs when running. The only disadvantage is that any attempt at dignity when wearing the harness detached from the glider is doomed to failure; you will look like some bizarre prehistoric lizard. This will not deter the keen pilot!

Some rigid harnesses have been produced in the USA, but the performance benefits are slight compared with the problems of carriage and durability, and their use has so far been confined to a small number of the keenest

Pilot and glider are well streamlined. The 'Bullet' type of harness leaves the legs well clear for a good run

Rich Pfeiffer models his own design of lightweight cocoon harness, with parachute and ballast compartments. Glider: Delta Wings 'Streak'

Chris Price's ingenious shell harness

A home-made french connection employed to ease roll control

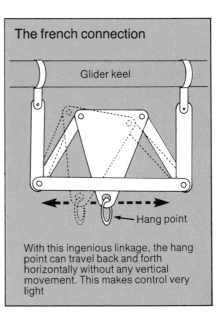

The french connection

Glider keel

Hang point

With this ingenious linkage, the hang point can travel back and forth horizontally without any vertical movement. This makes control very light

cross-country pilots flying the Owens Valley, USA.

Ballast containers
The competition pilot, engaged in a task which is a test of sheer speed, will often carry ballast as a means of temporarily increasing his wing loading. Some of the better soaring harnesses are available with an optional compartment for ballast. This is a really worthwhile extra, whether you wish to use it filled with dry sand as was intended for the contest flier, or just to carry your glider bag, sandwiches, book, first

aid kit, extra clothing etc., as the rest of us do.

The french connection
This is a beautifully simple device which has the function of reducing the effort the pilot has to input to influence either roll or pitch. The invention of Jean-Louis Darlet, the layout of the connection can best be seen in the illustrations. As the pilot moves, the point at which he is effectively connected to the glider moves also, supplementing his control input.

The commonest application in Britain is for the connection to be fitted in line with the keel, which

makes it less tiring to fly at speed for sustained periods. A supplementary benefit is that at high speeds the pilot's body remains more parallel with the airflow and so induces less drag. This can yield another mile an hour or so at top speed.

On gliders which are very heavy in roll, the connection may be fitted laterally. This is more common in the Alps than in the UK.

The ultimate refinement of the french connection is the Double Darlet which is basically two units joined at right angles to each other, thus lightening both roll and pitch effort.

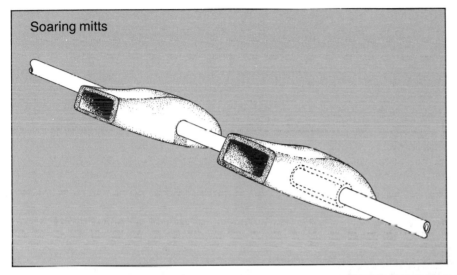

Soaring mitts

A pair of soaring mitts fitted to the control bar can make all the difference when long periods are to be spent flying at high altitude or during the winter. The best are made from closed-cell neoprene, and incorporate a tube of the same material around the bar, so that the pilot's hands are completely insulated from the cold aluminium

The addition of a french connection is a modification to the glider, and must not be undertaken lightly. Always consult the manufacturer of your wing before fitting one, and then have the installation checked out by a highly experienced flier. Bear in mind that you will not be receiving such strong feedback from the glider in the air, and take extra care about airspeed until you have completely adjusted to the revised feel of the aircraft.

Because more pivot points mean more wear points, there are more potential points of suspension failure, so no one should use a french connection without a strong, free running, back-up loop as well.

Navigation equipment

Compasses

Although compasses are carried on hang gliders, they tend not to be as effective as may at first be imagined. The technique of covering distances by constantly circling in thermals usually means that the compass rarely has the chance to settle down and give a true reading during flight. As our aircraft carry no power source from

'Double Darlet' french connection on Steve Moyes' 1983 World Championship-winning glider

which to energise gyroscopic instruments, we will have to accept the limitations of the magnetic variety for the foreseeable future, and use them as an overall guide rather than an accurate navigational device.

However, a magnetic compass is very useful on the ground before a flight, used in conjunction with a map. First an accurate check is taken on the wind direction, and due allowance made for alteration with height. This information is then transferred to the map where it may well show that a slight crosswind leg at some stage during the projected flight will take the flier over better soaring country, or keep him in contact with a retrieve route.

Maps

As your flying develops, your need for maps increases. When learning to soar, the sketch maps of your club's sites are all that is required. With luck that stage will not continue too long, and you will then have to invest in something more elaborate. In fact, you will rapidly discover that you need at least two maps. The first is an Aeronautical Chart, which shows where you can fly without encountering restricted airspace, danger zones, airports, glider ports and the host of other hazards which at first sight make the ICAO charts look rather daunting. The best Aeronautical

British Team pilot Graham Hobson. Note the map case on the bottom bar. Glider: Magic III

Chart to buy is the 1:500,000 series which gives a scale of approximately 8 miles to the inch. The second map you will need is an Ordnance Survey 1:50,000 (1¼ miles per inch) map of the immediate flying district, which you can use to plan your first trip away from the launch site.

As your cross-country flying becomes more ambitious, the large scale OS map may be replaced with one of the Routemaster Series at 1:250,000 scale (4 miles to the inch); these still have quite good contour representation, but allow a flight of many miles before falling off the edge of the map!

Although map reading in the air will become important as your flying advances, it is equally important to familiarise yourself with them on the ground. This preparation is a vital part of successful cross-country flying.

Advanced gliders

Almost any hang glider designed after 1976 will have an acceptable soaring performance in good ridge-lift conditions. Minimum-sink rates have not been greatly improved upon for some years. The big strides have been made in extending the speed range of the aircraft and producing much flatter glide angles at high speed. This

means that the pilot of later machines can fly more quickly through areas of sink while still being able to slow right down when taking advantage of lift. Thus the potential for cross-country flight is much greater.

The increase in useful top speeds from below 30 mph to over 50 mph in a few years has been achieved through minimising drag by cleaning up the design of the glider; increasing the *aspect ratio*, which makes the wing more efficient; and introducing sophisticated double-surface airfoil sections, the shape of which is accurately controlled by plastic inserts and pre-formed battens.

In aviation every step of progress seems to generate many extra problems, so we will look at how the designers have overcome some of the difficulties.

Minimising drag

First the sail is cut with a minimum of billow so that it will not flap at speed. Battens are placed where they will be most effective in preventing wrinkles and ripples while keeping the airfoil in shape. Any part of the airframe which does not contribute to lift or stability is either concealed, streamlined or reduced to the minimum section compatible with retaining adequate strength.

The most obvious drag-inducers

are the glider's main cross tubes. Several designs dispensed with these altogether, notably the Gryphon, Sigma, Emu and Sealander, but as a number of extra rigging wires became necessary to maintain the flight configuration, overall drag was not much reduced.

The big breakthrough came in 1980 with the introduction in the USA of Ultralight Products' Comet, designed by Roy Haggard. Haggard increased the area of the wing's double surfaces and concealed the cross tubes between them. That alone guaranteed enhanced performance, but if the then normal practice of bolting the cross tubes rigidly to the keel had been maintained, the resulting wing would have been too rigid to be turned using weightshift control. It must have required rare vision to adopt the not-so-obvious solution of letting the cross tubes float laterally, restrained only by a slack wire bridle.

This design worked so well that it became the father of the whole generation of gliders known today as CFX models, CFX standing for 'Concealed Floating Crossbooms'.

Kingposts and control-frame side tubes are frequently of streamlined section on high-performance gliders, and rigging wires are no longer always sheathed in plastic. The uneven surface of stranded stainless-steel cable generates less

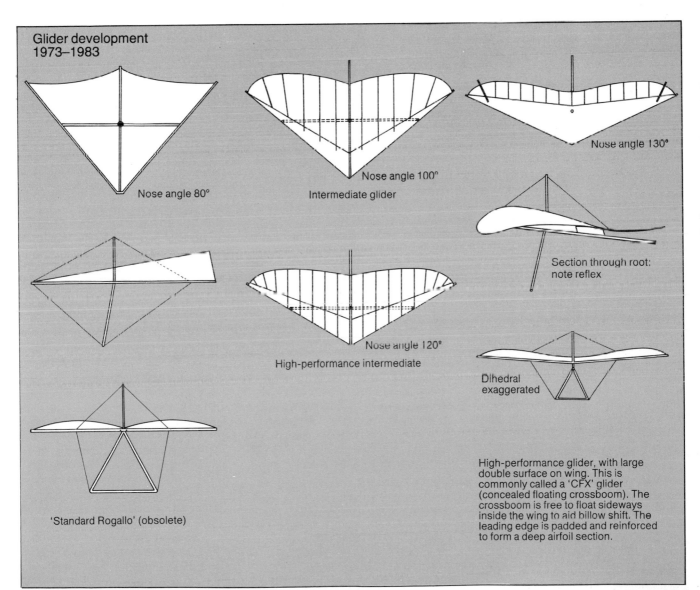

Glider development 1973–1983

Nose angle 80°

Nose angle 100°
Intermediate glider

Nose angle 130°

Section through root: note reflex

Nose angle 120°
High-performance intermediate

Dihedral exaggerated

'Standard Rogallo' (obsolete)

High-performance glider, with large double surface on wing. This is commonly called a 'CFX' glider (concealed floating crossboom). The crossboom is free to float sideways inside the wing to aid billow shift. The leading edge is padded and reinforced to form a deep airfoil section.

drag than a smooth, but necessarily thicker, coated cable.

All these small drag savings combine to make a significant contribution to glide efficiency at speed.

Because much of the frame of these gliders is concealed, extra care must be taken with pre-flight checking. The terminal points of cables and all the associated nuts and bolts must be inspected, even if it means much more peering and squinting inside the sail than is demanded by simpler models.

Raising the aspect ratio

The *aspect ratio* (A/R) of a wing is the relationship between span and average chord. Thus a wing of high

aspect ratio will be very long and thin when viewed from above. Provided that a suitable airfoil section can still be accommodated, such a wing will generate more lift than the more chunky type. Naturally designers seek to increase the A/R as far as is practicable. As usual there are problems: pitch stability becomes harder to provide: roll control becomes more difficult as the span increases: the leading edge tubes are subjected to ever greater loads, and so must be thicker and therefore heavier. This introduces more inertia, which further adversely affects handling.

In spite of the problems, we now have weightshift-controlled gliders

The Guggenmos 'Bullet' glider at the 1983 World Championships. An ultra-lightweight high-aspect-ratio machine

with aspect ratios in the region of 8:1 which still retain acceptable flying characteristics.

Defining the airfoil

Basic hang gliders depend on the pressure of the air to keep the wing in shape while flying. This is a very elegant solution to the problem of designing a readily foldable wing, but shortcomings become apparent as soon as one attempts to make such a wing move quickly through the air. It will deform and the airfoil will lose its efficiency before much speed is gained.

The cure is to define the section

using pre-formed battens in both surfaces. Then all along the leading edge a broad mylar strip is inserted into the sail which prevents it from sagging between the batten ribs while also preserving a good radius at the front of the section. Mylar is a very resilient plastic sheeting which is much used in the garment industry to prevent the lapels of your suit or waistband of your skirt from curling.

Mylar is also used in other ways on high-performance wings. It is a very smooth substance, with a great resistance to stretching. Used as a 'sandwich filling', bonded to lightweight woven sailcloth, it provides a sail which can be tightened up to an extreme degree of tune which it will then retain for a duration which ordinary cloth would not. Alternatively, as an outer layer on sailcloth it offers a very shiny ripple-free surface. This may be used either over the entire upper surface of the wing or over just the forward third.

The problem of stopping a high-A/R wing from pitching down and becoming stabilised in a dive is met by ensuring that some *reflex* is maintained in the section. *Leech lines* are run from the trailing edge to the top of the kingpost, while near the tips *anti-dive rods* control

Robert Bailey's Magic III shows just how flat and tight the sail on a modern wing can be. Mylar coating gives the glossy surface

the amount of possible downward movement.

Handling a high-performance hang glider

The latest gliders are not 'mean beasts', but the enhanced performance does demand more from the pilot in many ways. On the ground they are more exhausting to carry, and take a little longer to rig. The complex sails must be stowed with care if their appearance and performance are to be retained, and the batten profiles must be checked against the drawings at very frequent intervals.

To permit the floating crossboom to do its job of allowing relative movement when the pilot shifts his weight, the rigging on a CFX glider is slacker than on the less sophisticated wings. When in flight, the upper rigging is unloaded and therefore sloppy, but on the ground the loads are reversed, and the bottom wires are slack. This makes the whole aircraft feel very 'vague' when trying to get stabilised before takeoff, and newcomers to these wings can find it a little unnerving. The effect soon wears off.

In the air the CFX should be a delight to fly, with handling little different to the better intermediate gliders. If the sail is excessively tight, roll control may be slow and heavy. Competition pilots will fly with a very tight sail in the quest for speed at the expense of handling. Newcomers to CFXs will get on better with the glider in a 'soft' state of tune, and should be in no hurry to 'wind it up'.

Landing does require extra care. Although minimum stall speed will probably only be a mile an hour or so more than that of an intermediate glider, the inertia added by the heavier wing above you, plus the flatter glide angle, can make a large landing field seem rather small. Be prepared to plan your landing approaches much more carefully. Then control your speed over the ground by very gradually increasing the angle of attack and so bleeding the speed off. Finally flare out very positively with the hands quite high on the side tubes. The big trap to avoid is flaring out too soon: you will just convert speed into height and find that your 'landing' has been executed 15–20 ft (5–6 m) above the ground, and you have little choice but to stall the rest of the way. Expensive, painful and undignified. The fast, flat approach to landing will demonstrate *ground effect* very clearly. This is when you seem to fly on and on across the field with your control bar only a foot or so above the grass. What happens is that a cushion of air is formed between the wings and the ground which augments the lift and so enhances the glide. Flying straight in ground effect is fine, but any attempt to turn is almost certainly doomed. The proximity of the ground interferes with the complex flow of vortices around the wingtips. If this happens unevenly, as during a turn, the lower tip will almost inevitably stall.

Other high-performance gliders

As this is being written there is no doubt a designer somewhere planning a foot-launched aircraft which will make the CFX as obsolete as the Rogallos of a decade ago.

Hang gliders with a greater performance do already exist, but have not yet gained acceptance, because there are difficulties of portability, cost, handling and fragility.

7. Advanced flying

The first cross-country—'going for it'

Many recreational hang-glider pilots are content to confine their flying to exploiting ridge lift to the limit. Indeed, soaring the length of a reasonable ridge can be a very fulfilling experience, particularly on a smooth day when one can relax almost totally while becoming familiar with the patterns in the fields or watching ant-like traffic on the roads below. Wildlife is often completely oblivious to your silent presence above, and it can be fascinating to plot the course of a fox across the moortops or spot grouse making their strange, fast, ground-skimming flights a hundred feet below.

But on a day when thermals are active the ambitious pilot will want to exploit their power to the full, and that normally means waving goodbye to the security of the ridge and travelling back downwind with the rising air. In fliers' parlance this decision to leave the ridge is 'going XC' or even just 'going for it'.

Leaving the ridge for the first time is very much easier said than done. Some fliers manage without any problems, but most will admit that it was a real effort. There is a quite natural fear of landing in an unknown field, plus the worry that one will be 'sunk out' behind the hill and only achieve a mile or so across country, yet still have to endure all the problems of getting oneself and glider back to the car.

There can be few honest pilots who have been in a good thermal at decision point behind the ridge, and have not managed to find an urgent need to fly out of the thermal and return to the edge. 'The family is waiting in the car', or 'I don't think I have any change for the phone' are both reasons good enough to make one hesitate on that final, critical 360° and lose lift. Of course, once out of it you can fly back down and make quite a convincing display of bemoaning your ill fortune.

If the terrain is suitable, one good way of overcoming this psychological barrier and building up cross-country experience is by making the first attempt down the ridge and then back around the end. You may well have been able to inspect a potential landing field previously. It is unlikely that this approach will result in a big mileage first time, but it is a great confidence-builder.

A typical first flight
Let us share the experience of a pilot making a first cross-country flight over typical British moorland country. It is late Spring. Our example pilot holds a P2 certificate and flies in a relaxed style which never gives his fellow clubmen an anxious moment on the ridge. His flight today is going to be his best yet, not just because there is lots of good thermal activity, but also because he has done his preparations properly. This started maybe months ago, when he bought an air map of the area and began making flights of fancy along different tracks according to the wind directions prevailing at his club's sites.

Recently he became aware that he was flying forward out of thermal lift more and more often, and on one occasion had let himself get so far downwind that he had been unable to penetrate all the way back to the take-off point, landing a few hundred metres behind it. It only took one of his friends to say 'we thought you had gone for it that time', to make him regret not trying, although if the truth were known he was not really ready. He then just had a variometer, and had been obeying its warbled commands for some months, but today will be the first trial of his new altimeter. Also, since that comment on the hill a couple of weeks earlier, he has spent more time with his 1:500,000 air map. He now knows for certain that the only obstacle he may possibly encounter is an airfield special rules zone (SRZ) about 50 km away, just beyond a motorway. This morning he took the trouble to telephone the general aviation

weather service. From that he is armed with the knowledge that there is an unstable air mass over the part of the country containing his proposed site. He was told the height of freezing level, from which he could see that the lapse rate would be high, and also the wind direction and strength at 2,500, 5,000 and 7,500 ft. This all confirmed his hope and apprehension that he was in for a good XC day.

Rigging seems to take longer than usual. Several gliders are working the ridge: sometimes most of them seem quite low down, then at one edge of the ridge he will see a couple that seem to be mere specks—2,000 ft up at a guess. Time to fly.

When our pilot launches he is a little surprised that the wind is rather crossed from his left—when he arrived at the site it appeared to be square on. His launch is clean, but the lift does not feel quite as positive as usual with a 16 mph breeze on this particular site. Never mind, at least he is not going down; and after a short beat to the left he turns carefully and flies again past his takeoff point. He is conscious that he has a slight tailwind and is still only level with his launch, when suddenly the control bar feels almost as if it is alive in his hands. The vario immediately starts to scream and he instinctively hauls in

on the bar for a second or so before realising he should push out to achieve the best climb. His initial surprise soon passes, and he carries on along the ridge for a little longer, the vario still singing up, up, up. He knows he wants to stay in this powerful lift, and his next 180° turn is almost automatic, as is the one after that. Surely this is the best thermal he has ever connected with! The gliders on the ground at the launch site now look quite small, and he wants to make a 360° turn to stay within the thermal, but suddenly there seems to be a lot to do. He is aware of a red and blue glider not too far away, but he feels ashamed of himself when he realises that since connecting with the lift he has been staring at his vario needle to the exclusion of almost everything else. Was there more than one other glider close by? He dare not 360° until he has had another good look around. And how high was he? He tries to read his new altimeter but can't make much sense of its unfamiliar dial. Never mind—plenty of height now for a 360°, so another good look around the sky. Satisfied that there really is only that one other glider with him, he rolls his machine into a tightish turn and hears that the vario note hardly changes all the way round. He is too busy keeping a lookout to watch the needle this time, somehow trying to

compensate for his earlier lapse. All clear. Several more revolutions follow quite naturally. He can see the red and blue glider far below him now, and feels quite alone. Time to have another attempt at making sense of that altimeter. 2,100 ft? Impossible, surely. Then he realises that he forgot to set the instrument before takeoff. He reasons that he must be about 2,000 ft higher than his home, where he probably last zeroed the needle. That means if he deducts the height of the hill—about 800 ft, he remembers—then he has made 1,200 ft already. Or should he *add* the height of the hill? While most of his brain is occupied with these inconclusive mental exercises, enough grey cells are left over to monitor the vario (which is still pointing upwards), and to send out instructions for more 360°s.

The last 360° is the critical one. He transfers his attention to the launch area and the edge of the ridge. They are as far off as they had been the day he had had to carry back a couple of weeks earlier. 'Oh well,' he thinks, 'I'm pretty sure I'm higher this time, so I can get back from this 360°, and as I'm still climbing I'll no doubt be able to get back from the next one if need be.' But he is wrong this time. As it goes higher, his thermal is also travelling over the ground more quickly,

The anatomy of a tight 360°:

(1) Pulling on speed. Pilot has weight right through bar

(2) Weightshift across bar—still lots of speed

(3) Pushing out and centralising on bar. Angle of bank established

(4) A quarter of the way round. Pilot hasn't moved

(5) Halfway. Pilot hasn't moved

(6) Threequarters. Pilot still hasn't moved

(7) Almost complete. Note re-appearance of launch area

(8) Rolling out. Pilot moving to opposite corner and angle of bank reducing. Simultaneously pulling on some speed again. *Note*: If the turn had been perfectly executed, the pilot's body would have been in line with the keel throughout

96

8

7

6

because of the wind gradient. One more 360° demonstrates this quite clearly. Like it or not, our pilot realises that he has indeed 'gone for it' at last! A sudden feeling of confusion, bordering on panic, overtakes him, and for a moment or two he tries to select suitable downwind landing fields. No sooner is he up than he is thinking about getting down again! But then he remembers the times he has looked at the map; he concentrates again on keeping his glider circling in the lift while realising that if he just carries on in a straight glide away from his takeoff point, he will land on the far side of the farm below. Another few turns and he is sure he will be able to clear the village, and that would be nearly five miles. He is by now both elated and very tense. Hardly realising it, ever since he connected with the thermal he has been gripping the control bar as if he wished to crush it. Now he becomes aware that his hands are aching, and he has only been airborne for about fifteen minutes. He makes a conscious effort to relax, and is rewarded by being pitched into some quite strong turbulence, whereupon the vario goes silent. No doubt he has lost the thermal and is in the sinking air surrounding it. He pulls on a little speed, makes a tight 180° turn, and flies straight back into the thermal. As he feels the nose of the glider

surge up, he eases the bar out and starts counting—one . . . two . . . three . . . four. The vario chirps before 'one', and is still singing on 'four' so he starts to 360° again. And that he continues to do all the way to cloudbase.

He begins to feel rather pleased with himself. Then the first foggy white wisps of cloud flick beneath his gloved fingers, and the control bar tugs again. Rapidly his downward view becomes hazy, the air becomes rougher, and he is immediately certain that for now he does not wish to venture one inch higher! Not only has he reached cloudbase, he is now rapidly reaching into cloud. Going up was fine, but he realises that arriving there is damp, cold, and possibly illegal. He wants out, but even pulling on full speed only drags the vario needle back to nil, and as soon as he relaxes the pressure at all, up it goes again. By now all he can distinguish on the ground is an occasional glint from the river in the sunlight.

All the horror stories about being sucked up into towering cumulo-nimbus flash through his mind, while he keeps the glider diving at full speed. He thinks of trying a spiral dive, but rejects the idea in favour of flying straight on, in the hope of outspeeding his now hostile cloud. After less than a minute he is back in sunlight once

again. But it is certainly more than a minute before he has recovered his composure sufficiently to think about making the most of his flight once more. All this time the vario has been indicating a steady '4-down'.

His encounter with the cloud has made him conscious of the distribution of the clouds in the sky, and he takes notice of the pattern their shadows make on the ground as they march down the now shallow valleys and across the plain. The certainty that he will also reach the plain reassures him, and his previous apprehension about landing places becomes much less. Still his vario shows a steady loss of 300–400 ft per minute, but just after he passes over a small town he feels the now familiar surge as his wings enter a rising column of air. The vario sings at once. He counts to four and starts to turn, only to be rudely pitched forward as the glider and he go 'over the falls' and seem to be momentarily weightless. He is well into his flight by now and determined to get into this particular thermal even if it has rejected him the first time. He speeds up a little, makes a crisp turn and flies back into where it should be. Right first time! He banks into his initial 360° a little sooner, and is rewarded by a climbing turn all the way round. This thermal proves even stronger than the first—the day is a little older and

An expert in action. Dean Kupchanko (Canada) amid the
Bavarian Alps

the sun now warmer—and he feels as if he were being flown upwards following the inside of some enormous invisible factory chimney. He hardly has to adjust his turns at all. The thermal almost seems to tell the glider where it needs to be for best effect. A 2,000-ft height gain takes hardly any time, and at 6,000 ft by his altimeter he pulls speed on again to avoid another cloud encounter.

He now expects to be able to find another thermal almost on demand, but it is not to be so easy again. He concentrates on flying at what feels like the best glide angle, but 200 to 300 down is the result each time. He still seems quite high up, but his altimeter tells him he is down to his takeoff height again: he has ground clearance only because the plain is so much lower than the launch hill had been.

He starts to think seriously about the ground again, as selection of a landing site becomes a prime consideration. Altering course a few degrees to the right puts him on the same side of the river as the road. It also takes him over a single ploughed field which, being darker, had throughout that morning absorbed more solar energy than its neighbours. The air above the field has also naturally become warmer and less dense than that surrounding it, and started to float upwards. Then cooler air flows in to

take its place, and this is causing quite a lot of local turbulence. Our pilot feels the turbulence, then his right wing is pushed upwards as it enters the newborn thermal, and his glider turns rapidly to the left. He hangs on and eventually gets the wings level before searching out the lift. But this time it is not going to be anything like as easy as before. He gets three-quarters of the way around a 360° before being spat out again, and sometimes he feels as if he were riding a bicycle over a motocross track rather than flying. He gains about 800 ft before losing contact with the lift again. Maybe he is tiring a little now, and losing concentration. Certainly he is no longer sure of the true wind direction, which has a lot to do with it. He is never to find another thermal that day, but he does cover a further two miles before making a perfect landing in a large paddock, enduring the scrutiny of a handful of cows in one corner. He picked the field with great care: it was not quite the most convenient, but it was the biggest and contained the fewest animals. It appeared free of overhead wires and their telltale posts. He made his decision early enough to make a full circuit inside the boundaries, and prepared for a nil-wind landing as he could not detect any significant breeze. His final approach was naturally towards the direction from which he had

taken off, in the absence of any other clear indication of wind direction, and sure enough he touched down into about a 4 mph drift. Our pilot's first cross-country flight was concluded exactly twenty-one miles from takeoff!

The lessons
This imaginary first cross-country voyage did not go exactly according to the textbooks, but then they hardly ever do. For a first go he really did not do too badly—the mistake rate was about par for the course. Let's have a look at his errors:

Firstly, he did not realise that the slight crosswind at take-off was induced by a powerful thermal nearby, which was drawing air towards itself. It was only by good fortune that his beat took him into that thermal, whereas a more experienced flier might well have been able to predict its presence from the wind-shift.

Secondly, during his pre-launch check he did not register the 'big picture' regarding the weather conditions. It takes a fair bit of time and experience to educate the eyes to take in all the information presented to them. At first there is a tendency to look out in front of the hill and take note only of the conditions directly ahead, and then just as far as they will affect the first few minutes of flight. The advanced

100

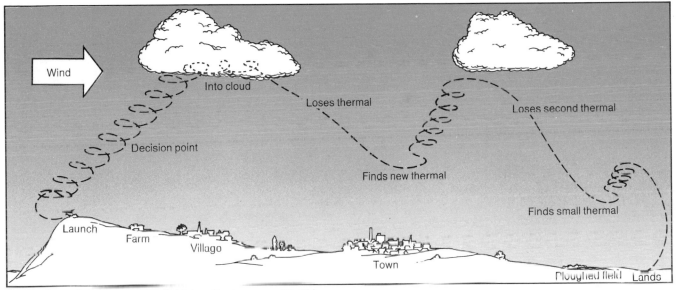

Wind

Into cloud

Loses thermal

Loses second thermal

Decision point

Finds new thermal

Finds small thermal

Launch

Farm

Village

Town

Ploughed field   Lands

The imaginary first cross-country flight described on pages 93–100

The imaginary first cross-country flight described on pages 93–100

pilot would automatically scan the whole view, from one side of the horizon to the other, and also take in the downwind scene. He would have known that small cumulus clouds were developing both in front and behind him, and that the sky was 'active' all over.

Then thirdly, he would have looked around himself all the time and been aware of the exact position of other gliders on the ridge. There is no excuse for not doing this. In hang gliding,

observation and survival are permanently interlocked.

The fourth mistake was not setting his altimeter before launch, but we will let him off this time because everyone forgets occasionally. With a bit more experience, our pilot will automatically set his altimeter needle to the height of the launch site as part of his pre-flight routine. Then he will know that all the altitudes he reads during the flight will be above mean sea level (amsl).

This system feels a little strange at first but it is worth getting used to it. Many pilots stick a label onto their varios with the heights of their popular club sites on it as a handy crib.

The fifth mistake was a fortuitous one, which actually launched him on his XC: he had overlooked the wind gradient, even though the weather report had told him that the windspeed at 5,000 ft was five knots more than at 2,500 ft.

We can hardly call his tenseness

during most of his flight a mistake. Only a rare and gifted flier will not tense up at some stage on early cross-country flights.

Being taken by surprise on entering the cloud was a mistake: he should have known it was imminent. With more experience he will learn to direct his last few 360°s towards the sunny side of the clouds, and will often find he is able to climb up the side for several hundred more feet.

After his cloud experience he managed rather well; only more cross-country airtime will increase his thermal-hunting skill. It is worth bearing in mind that a very slight adjustment of direction can often make a tremendous difference to the ease of retrieve. A stream which looks totally insignificant from 500 ft will become quite an obstacle at ground level if it is between you and the road.

The overall lesson is that the best way to learn cross-country is to do it: our pilot did more pure learning on his big flight than he would ever have achieved by just reading the theory. However, without some basic groundwork the whole episode could well have been a disaster. The mapwork beforehand is essential. A beginner at XC who strays into controlled airspace a few miles downwind may well be endangering the lives of many. No one begins to qualify as an

advanced flier without first becoming a responsible one.

Mountain flying

Assuming you have good basic hang gliding skills and plenty of confidence, then sooner or later you will want to taste the undisputed delights of flying really high in the mountains. This section should speed the learning process.

So far we have been concerned with advanced flying from a typical British site. Only in the wilder parts of North Wales and Scotland do alpine conditions exist in the UK, and then usually without the profusion of chairlifts and cable cars which make top access so much easier in countries with developed winter-sports areas. Let us consider what is involved in flying, say, in the Alps.

Big mountain flying is surely one of the great experiences of hang gliding. All the sensations are greater than those to which a hill flier is accustomed, and in many ways so are the dangers. Preparation becomes extra important, and a parachute is really essential. (In some countries, such as West Germany, it is also a statutory requirement.) Your harness has to be properly adjusted and comfortable as there is not usually any opportunity to land back on top to alter it.

The yellow parachute bridle-strop shows well in this alpine shot. Glider: Solar 'Storm'

Top: Alpine landing approach at Hohenschwangau, Bavaria

Below: A group share a thermal in the Bavarian Alps

A pilot who has gained his airtime by soaring ridges a few hundred feet high will probably find his early mountain flights a mind-blowing experience. He will have difficulty in adjusting to the vast change in scale, and he will also find that existing on thermals alone, usually without the comfort of a top-landable ridge to which to return, can initiate a strange feeling of being 'cast adrift'.

This is not the place for pilots with less than Pilot 2 capabilities. If you do not yet have the experience to fly your machine so that the wing seems to respond to your thoughts rather than by considered physical input, then you are not yet ready for the Alps.

Before launching
Talk to the local fliers. Quite apart from the obvious matter of courtesy, this precaution may well save your neck. At some of the 'big name' European sites this could turn out to be rather easier said than done. Do not assume that just because the pilot you have met has the very latest equipment and speaks English with a French accent he is necessarily an expert on that mountain. He may well be an affable Belgian who arrived yesterday and has an extensive

knowledge only of soaring coastal sand-dunes!

Mountain weather alone is complex enough to warrant a book to itself, and its effects are often magnified in proportion to the size of the mountains themselves. If the locals are not launching it is probably because they have developed respect for the conditions the hard way. Leave the heroics for another day if this is the case.

Mountain launches
Basically there are three types of launch: the normal running takeoff from a slope, the ramp launch and the cliff launch.

The mountain running takeoff
The running takeoff differs from that described in Chapter 3 in one important respect: you will have to be going faster because the air will be thinner. Mix in the likelihood that the run-off area consists of eroded rocks and stones, and that little thermals may be popping up any time, and you will understand that the scope for ending your flying holiday before it has got off the ground is quite considerable. The casual lope that so easily gets you airborne off the English South Downs, for instance, simply will not work at 8,000 ft. In fact, the true difference in airspeed required is only about 2 mph over an 8,000 ft

Just airborne off the ramp at St Hilaire. Note the angle of the end of the ramp to the right of the picture

Plenty of helpers at this contest ramp. Note keelman

The ramp launch

height differential. This may not sound much, but in all probability you will be taking off into much lighter winds than you are accustomed to, so the need for an accurately planned and powerful run is clear. The trick, as usual, is to start slowly and accelerate throughout the run; avoid at all costs the temptation to flop down into the harness when you think you are going fast enough. The wing must take you off the ground when it is ready, and there is no way you will persuade it otherwise. The cost of attempting to will surely be bent uprights and skinned knees.

A light wind launch from a well designed ramp is really extremely easy, although it certainly presents the first-timer with an unrivalled thrill. Ramps come in all shapes and sizes. The best of them run close to the hill and are very steep. Other examples range from square-edged concrete constructions which seem to be so placed as to maximise local turbulence, to some which are like sections of a seaside pier built horizontally over treetops. We will deal with the latter varieties later. Let us concentrate on a well-designed steep ramp first, such as that built at St Hilaire du Touvet, near Grenoble, scene of the 1979 World Championships. It is quite a small wooden construction, perhaps two metres wide and five metres long, pointing downwards at an angle of 45 degrees. It is almost impossible not to make a good clean launch off this ramp, which is just as well because it projects over a sheer cliff some 1,500 ft high.

The technique is simple: stand on the small horizontal platform at the

105

A Comet II clears the Tegelberg ramp.
The lake is about 2,750 ft (800 m) below

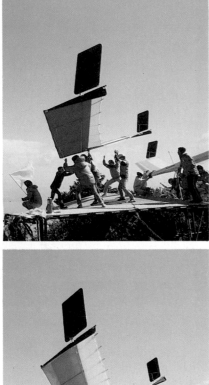

The flapping flags are evidence enough that
the energetic ground-handling crew is
essential to help this class 2 glider to launch
safely

A US team pilot at only 16 years old, Chris Bulger uses flying mitts permanently attached to the bottom bar. Glider: Delta Wings 'Streak'

Ramp launch—halfway: the glider is flying, but not yet developing sufficient lift to hoist the pilot too. Howard Vandall of Canada on a UP Comet II

top of the ramp, and lift the glider to the 'straps tight' position. Not only does this provide for the best pitch control, it also gives final confirmation that the pilot is indeed clipped in. Then advance so that the toes are just overhanging the top of the ramp proper, check wings are level, and nudge the glider forwards from the shoulders. As the wing gathers speed it becomes immediately quite automatic to take the few steps down the ramp which are all that is necessary before finding oneself soaring free with the cliffs receding behind.

There really is no more to it than that. However, the foregoing description leaves out the psychological factor. We are the first generation of humans to have the opportunity of running off the equivalent of a henhouse roof a quarter of a mile high, and there are those among us whose minds are not yet totally adjusted to the procedure. Most, in fact. Here are some tips to help overcome the knocking-knees syndrome.

1 If you get a feeling of vertigo on first inspecting the ramp without your wings, don't worry, you are in good company. More than one prominent British Team member suffers in the same way. It will be quite different when clipped into your glider.
2 Do a meticulous pre-flight including hang check while in the rigging area behind the ramp, before carrying forward.
3 Make a point of repeating the hang check at the ramp-top platform even if nobody else seems to be bothering, and there are a dozen other fliers in the queue behind.
4 Do not complicate your first ramp launch with glider-mounted cameras etc. Leave that for later flights—you have enough to occupy yourself for now.
5 Avoid launching just behind another glider—you do not want to enter wake turbulence.
6 Do not concentrate on the far end of the ramp. Before starting your
108

run, check that air is clear in the normal manner, then look out to each wingtip for a second or so. Now look down at where your first footstep will be, then concentrate on the mountains on the other side of the valley and GO!
7 Your first ramp-launched mountain flight is now under way. Relax into your harness and set about enjoying the thermal search.

Flatter ramps
Broadly speaking, the more shallow the ramp the more difficult the launch, particularly in very light air. You will know from experience on home sites that a nil-wind takeoff from a shallow hill requires very accurate control of pitch during the run. The same is of course true on a shallow ramp, with the added feature that the ramp has an end out in space. As you stand on it you realise that it is positively finite. At this point it will occur to the thinking pilot that if he has not got his act together before reaching the far end, he is hardly likely to enjoy his day.
    The slow start/steady acceleration rule applies as usual, but do not be afraid, towards the end of the ramp, to keep the nose at a slightly lower angle of attack than would be usual, and actually be prepared almost to dive off the end. In practice, if your run has been positive, the dive will be virtually

non-existent—merely a slight loss of height while speed is built up. The trap to avoid is pushing out at the ramp end and thus launching stalled. This is by far the most common form of ramp takeoff accident, and can be easily avoided if the run is thought through and executed properly.

Concrete ramps
These demand great respect because they always seem to have sharp edges which are natural generators of local turbulence. Usually the cliff-launch technique is necessary and the pilot should think long and hard before deciding on an unassisted run-off.

Cliff launches
Before discussing the mechanics of a cliff-top takeoff, let us clearly understand the problems. The air is flowing *up* the face of the mountain. The hang glider pilot wishes to launch from a ledge at the top into this vertical airflow. At that very same point the air finds that it is no longer directed vertically by the cliff, but is free to make its own arrangements again. A large proportion of the airflow does indeed continue on upwards, but a significant amount curls over the top of the cliff and generates a strong local rotor. Problem one is to rig, pre-flight check and get the glider to the launch position without

being caught out by the rotor. Problem two is that of successfully launching from a horizontal surface into vertical air without getting the wing into a monumental stall.

The answer to both problems is that help is needed: help which must understand the problems, and be properly co-ordinated. Most hang glider launch sites attract tourists and sightseers who are usually only too happy to lend a hand. However, the chances of them knowing precisely what to do and then acting in a co-ordinated manner are slight unless they are told. Your first responsibility is the safety of your helpers, but it is easy to forget this when the adrenalin is pumping just before takeoff.

Let us assume you have just rigged and are about to stand the glider on its control frame. Just because you always put the nose down facing takeoff at home, do not take it for granted that it will be the same here. In all probability the rigging area is in a wind shadow with the rotor generating occasional gusts from behind. In this case the glider is safer with the nose up and the keel resting on the ground. If in doubt, take your cue from the locals.

On the most tricky sites it may take four people, apart from the pilot, to effect a clean launch. First there must be a wire-man to hold the nose wires immediately prior to

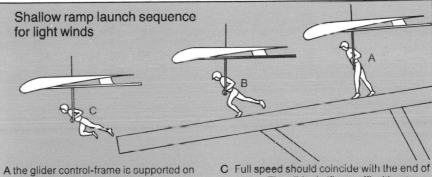

Shallow ramp launch sequence for light winds

A the glider control-frame is supported on the pilot's upper arms, and the control bar is kept well in towards the legs as the run commences.

B The run is well under way: the glider has risen to the 'straps tight' position. One hand may now be on the bottom bar, but care is taken to prevent the nose of the glider from rising.

C Full speed should coincide with the end of the ramp. The glider is 'flown off' without pushing the nose up and thus stalling. A dive after take-off cannot always be avoided, but a steady accelerating run down the ramp should minimise it.

Note: In stronger winds a suitable variation of the cliff-launch technique must be used. Wire-men are essential

Cliff technique: fresh wind

Note the very nose-down angle of attack. The wire-man is tied to the hill, and the keel-man is there only to protect the glider from rotor turbulence—*not* to push! Provided that the pilot takes up a position yielding a moderately high-speed cruise immediately on push-off, rotation of the nose up to a normal flying attitude will be automatic and virtually instantaneous.

launch. He will either be standing on a lower ledge or else kneeling right on the cliff edge. He will have his back to a long drop, so it is vital that he is roped to a sound belay for safety.

The pilot does not clip in until he has carried forward holding the nose wires, with the assistance of two side-wire men who keep the glider level while all the time *standing behind* their wires. That way they are not going to be accidentally pushed forwards at launch. Lastly, a keel man ensures that those treacherous rotor gusts do not flip the wing over from behind. The keel man should clearly understand that this duty is the limit of his responsibilities, and he is not there to give a hefty shove on takeoff—few actions are better calculated to complicate pitch control at a dangerous moment!

Once the nose-wire man has a firm hold, he should be reminded, 'do no let go until I shout RELEASE'. Then the pilot clips in, performs a meticulous hang check, and raises the control bar a few inches off the ground. Because of the nose-down attitude of the wing his view will be particularly poor, and he will have to rely on the nose-man to release him clear of other gliders.

If all is well, he checks and re-checks that the side wire-men are not exerting any real pressure to

A Class II glider launches in Japan. Roll control is via the moveable tip rudders. Glider: Fledgling

The cable car provides a civilised route to the launch area

Ready to launch using the 'straps tight' method. This is only possible in a strong wind where no run will be required. The wire-men should not be in this position at the edge of a steep cliff as they could be knocked over during a badly co-ordinated effort

◀ Harry Unsworth airborne off the big ramp at Whitwell, Tennessee. A cine camera is mounted on the keel. Glider: Birdman 'Cherokee'

A truckload of gliders in the Owens Valley, USA

keep the wings level—they should be aiding his judgement by holding their hands just off the wire if appropriate. Then it is time for a big swallow, call 'sidewires free', a moment of pause, then 'release'! An almost simultaneous forward thrust will have the glider soaring up and away in smooth vertical lift. At the moment of release the nose of the glider may have been pointing downwards at an angle of up to about 45 degrees, according to the wind strength. This is vital—as it moves forwards into the vertical airstream the glider will rapidly rotate into a normal flying attitude without any tendency to stall or be blown back. Attempts to fly out level are inevitably doomed: up goes the nose on release: forward speed is nil, as is directional control. Then one wing gets a little more into the airstream than the other, starts to fly and rotates the whole aircraft back into the mountain in an embryonic spin. A planned launch with a good nose-down attitude guarantees avoidance of that particular form of disaster.

Once off the ground in the mountains
For the first day or so the new mountain flier will probably be satisfied to stay in the region of his takeoff and concentrate on adjusting to the scale of his new environment. In areas where a 'sled

ride' from launch to landing may take a quarter of an hour, there is time to cover quite an area searching for thermal lift. All the pointers referred to in Chapter 4 apply in the mountains, adjusted for scale of course.

What is really important is that a flier used to smaller, smoother hills should rapidly learn how differently the wind appears to behave in the Alps. Certainly, well above the mountain tops—say a thousand feet or more—there will be a true wind

blowing. Below that height it is simpler to think of the air as 'flowing' through the valleys and around the mountains, much as water would flow through a labyrinth. Punctuate this complex flow with vertical components generated by both thermal and topographical influences and the pilot will begin to build up a picture of the subtleties of the air into which he is launching.

A wind sock or streamers on the landing field are especially valuable

The gliders standing tail-down at different angles are a sure sign of nil wind behind an alpine launch site

A bumpy approach to a mountain landing field. Speed is essential to maintain full control in conditions which may change from minute to minute

to the mountain flier. The flow effect can often produce a wind which is blowing up one valley but down the next, even though both lie on, say, an east/west axis. Moreover, strong thermal disturbances can result in 180° wind shifts which may catch out the most experienced pilot. Seek every clue you can as to wind direction —smoke, moving crops, water ripples, flags etc.—over at least the last half-mile or so to the landing field, and maintain a reasonably high speed right to flare-out. That way you will have a better chance of making substantial last-minute direction changes in the event of a wind shift.

Mountain cross-countries

Although it is a rather crude over-generalisation, there is some truth in the assertion that thermals most frequently follow a path up the sides of mountains, rather than popping straight up the middle of valleys. Now imagine a long spine-backed ridge with thermals being generated on both sides and occasionally meeting at the top. There is no wind. This is a classic situation of thermal convergence, and fortunate indeed is the hang-glider pilot who has launched into a thermal and manages to work it up until he is above the ridge: he

The Hiway 'Explorer' was a brave attempt at a high-performance Class II glider. Directional control is via the cable-operated spoilers just visible on the upper wing surfaces

A UP 'Comet' approaches the summit of Mt ▶ Yufu, Kyushu, Japan

may travel the length of it and back again, hopping from thermal to thermal, or he may voyage its length while gaining sufficient height to cross the valley to repeat the process along another ridge. This is the classic method of making long flights, be they free distance, out-and-return or triangular.

But if there is a breeze of any strength blowing onto that spine-backed ridge, then the approach has to be very different. Long flights are still possible, but it is a recipe for disaster to use the system our pilot employed at the beginning of this chapter. The rotor behind a large steep mountain is enormously powerful, and likely to be more than a match for a hang glider. Stay in front of the ridge and take no chances with being blown back into the rotor. Casually thermalling up a bit, then setting off 'over the back', is not the way to proceed! The absolute minimum is 1,000 ft clearance, and rather more is comfortable. Gaps need more respect as well. Have you ever noticed how there always seems to be a gale blowing through a mountain pass? Think about the 'flowing' effect and the reason is immediately understood: as the air goes through the narrow gap it speeds up. This also leads to the effect which fliers in the USA so

Note the tightness of the sail as Bulger gets safely away

graphically describe as 'canyon suck'. So give breaks in the mountains a wide berth—keep well forward, keep high, and try to maintain a mental picture of what the air is likely to be doing.

Balloon launches

The great American pioneer Montgomery organised many daring and successful flights of his gliders from hydrogen balloons in 1904–5, flights of up to eight miles being recorded. Balloonists have also frequently dropped parachutists at fetes and flying displays for the last hundred years or so. Needless to say it was not long before the modern generation of sporting hang glider fliers sought to try this spectacular way of obtaining launch height, beneath hot-air balloons.

Let it be said from the beginning that this exercise is not to be undertaken lightly. A high degree of competence on behalf of both balloon and glider pilot is essential, as is a reasonable understanding of each other's craft.

Murphy's celebrated law, that if anything can go wrong it will do, has ample scope for running riot wherever a balloon/hang glider combination is let loose. This is probably because the whole procedure is rather inconvenient for all the parties concerned. The

116

consolation is that when it does go off without a hitch one experiences a sensation of exhilaration and satisfaction which is quite unique.

If you ever find yourself likely to undertake a release from a balloon, then ponder the following. Firstly, you cannot just go out and do a balloon launch—the CAA must first grant a dispensation to the balloon pilot to drop from his aircraft anything other than ballast or articles for the saving of life. They will need assurance that the hang glider pilot is very experienced. If the launch is proposed as part of any public display then they will also require a rehearsal launch some days before the main event.

The process is on the face of it quite simple: tie the glider and pilot about 20 ft beneath the basket, hold the balloon down with groundlines while it is heated sufficiently to develop surplus lift, release the balloon slowly, maintaining control via groundlines until the strop to the glider is tight, then lift off and climb away. When ready for the launch, cool the balloon until a fairly high rate of descent is registering, and release the glider, which flies away serenely.

It is not until one is actively involved with a balloon-release operation that the enormity of the foul-up arena into which one has entered becomes apparent. None of the following examples are

imaginary, although the author would have to be very heavily bribed before publishing names!

Example 1
The ascent started in the lee of a building, with a wood downwind. As soon as the balloon cleared the building it naturally set off towards the trees. Unfortunately it was not high enough for the glider to clear the branches through which the hapless pilot found himself being dragged. Unsure of whether the glider was damaged or not, after a brief aerial conference it was decided to attempt to land without releasing the glider in the air. It will never be established how sound this decision was, because as soon as the glider touched the ground the balloon automatically became sufficiently bouyant to fly on its own. Glider and pilot were dragged for a considerable distance through hedges and ditches during which time it became very badly damaged. The balloon pilot had unfortunately dropped the knife with which he was to have released the glider, while the now mud-encrusted glider pilot felt that the best contribution he could make to the wellbeing of the expedition was to release his parachute. This had little effect beyond shredding the canopy.

Example 2
Ordinary rope was used to lift the glider. It untwisted as they rose and

Dawn lift-off for a balloon launch. Glider: Solar 'Storm'

the constant rotation made the hang glider pilot sick. The rest of the flight went without a hitch. Not so next time. To avoid the rotation problem, two ropes were used, one at the keel and one at the kingpost. Murphy's law being in operation, the kingpost rope was released first. That the glider righted itself from its eventual vertical release position owes rather more to luck than judgement.

Example 3

CB radio was (illegally) employed for communication between the pilots. It worked perfectly on the ground. As they rose, reception became possible for dozens of miles in all directions except over the 20 or so feet vertically between the glider and balloon. Both parties eventually resorted to shouting.

Example 4

A strong climatic inversion resulted in the balloon being unable to climb beyond a few hundred feet, owing to insufficient buoyancy. The glider pilot was eventually released at an uncomfortably low altitude and without any significant rate of descent, and then only after various solid objects had been thrown out of the basket past him in a desperate attempt to gain a few extra feet of height.

Yes, a balloon drop is always an event. If, after the preceding examples, you are still intent on going ahead, try these tips: check with the manufacturer of your glider—some are more pitch-stable than others, and you do not want to be in any doubt about this. Use tape and not rope with which to suspend the glider. Have some other hang-glider pilots in your handling crew who will understand your problems. The cheapest and most positive communication system between balloon and glider is a battery-powered wire intercom or baby alarm! Fit a jack-plug connector in the wire which will easily pull apart on release. Such systems are very cheap and seem foolproof, but remember that the lift tape will stretch on lift-off, so leave plenty of slack in the intercom wire. Do remember that even the simplest of release mechanisms can go wrong—if you are using a mechanical method, make sure that there is a sharp knife tied on somewhere handy in the balloon in case all else fails!

However executed, the actual release is, for the glider pilot at least, a moment of some drama. The ascent under the balloon is so gentle and smooth that the initial rude drop on launch results in a testing second of bladder control. Even if the balloonist has achieved a good rate of descent, this only inflates the wing—there is no forward speed whatsoever, so you

Dual hang check on top of Lookout Mountain

are setting off totally and completely stalled. The pilot's arms should be well braced, and approximately in the min-sink flying position. There is no need at all to pull on speed as gravity assumes responsibility for doing that. In fact, it has been waiting to take over for some time, and throws itself into the task with gusto. If the arms are not firmly braced there is a tendency for the pilot to drop forward through the control frame during that brief initial

downward rush.

After release, the flight down will probably be almost an anticlimax, but as everyone who has done it will tell you—'the only way to find out what a balloon drop is really like is to do one'.

Dual flying

In some countries—notably France—many people's first experience of our sport is a dual

'Togetherness is a dual launch'

flight from a mountain site, and indeed in Britain there was once a vogue for dual training. The development of the tethered teaching technique, which is more effective and much safer, rendered dual training obsolete. Some passenger flying still goes on, and in the right conditions it can be most enjoyable. Ideally you need a strongish wind, a large glider, and a site with easy top-landing.

The most common method is to use two prone harnesses side by side, with the passenger suspended about 8 to 10 in (20–25 cm) higher than the pilot. The pilot flies the glider in the normal way, while the passenger puts one arm around the pilot's back, holding lightly on the corner of the control bar with the other. The hang-point should be moved forwards up to 2 in (5 cm).

Plenty of practice and rehearsed hang checks are essential, and the pilot must be confident that the passenger understands everything that is going to happen and is unlikely to become rigid with fear at any stage! Make it clear that once the word 'Release' has been said at launch, there is no opportunity for a change of heart.

A top landing into a good breeze is much to be preferred; you will find that the price you pay for having someone to talk to in flight is a greatly increased stall speed, while

Getting into thermals

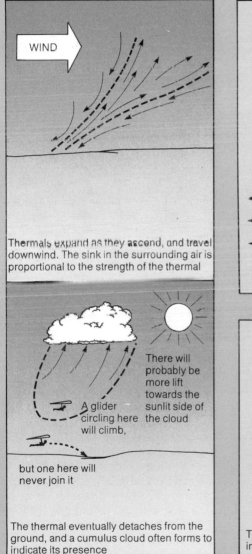

Thermals expand as they ascend, and travel downwind. The sink in the surrounding air is proportional to the strength of the thermal

There will probably be more lift towards the sunlit side of the cloud

A glider circling here will climb,

but one here will never join it

The thermal eventually detaches from the ground, and a cumulus cloud often forms to indicate its presence

Plan view of thermal

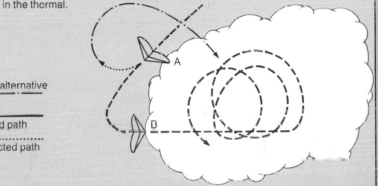

In this example, the left wingtip enters the thermal lift at A which immediately rolls the glider to the right, i.e. away from the lift. The pilot's reaction should be to swing his legs towards the thermal, then initiate a positive turn to enter the lift squarely at B. After the entry, he should fly straight for three or four seconds before starting to circle within the lift.

Note: Because of the need to turn at very short notice, the thermal-seeking pilot must always be aware of the position of other gliders with which he may be sharing the air. He should always make his 360° turns in the direction established by gliders already in the thermal.

Possible alternative path

Corrected path

Uncorrected path

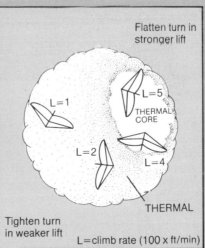

Flatten turn in stronger lift

L=5

THERMAL CORE

L=1

L=2

L=4

THERMAL

Tighten turn in weaker lift

L=climb rate (100 x ft/min)

Lift in a thermal is rarely uniform across it. The successful pilot will not be content with simply staying in lift, but will be constantly probing to locate the thermal core. A good technique is to alter the angle of bank, and therefore the radius, during each circle. If the turn is tightened where the vario shows weaker lift and widened when stronger is indicated, the core should eventually be found. Because each thermal has a different character, much practice and experience are vital to exploit their energy to the full

A good dual launch from the concrete ramp

their extra drag will do no good at all for the sink rate. The alternative will be executing a running landing on an aircraft which goes down quicker and lands faster than any you have previously dealt with. And as if that were not enough, you have someone else shackled to the thing as well. Yes, dual fliers must be prepared to look upon the occasional control frame upright as being expendable.

Taking someone else into the air gives you a burden of responsibility you have not previously borne. It is not something to tackle for the fun of it on the spur of the moment. If you do decide to do it, think each flight through carefully and fly with an even greater margin of safety than usual—you owe that to your partner.

Insurance for dual flying

Carrying a passenger on a glider may invalidate your third party insurance. You will need clearance from the manufacturer that your machine is suitable for the task, and capable of withstanding the extra loads two people will impose on it.

Check with both your manufacturer and the BHGA office or their insurers before flying dual.

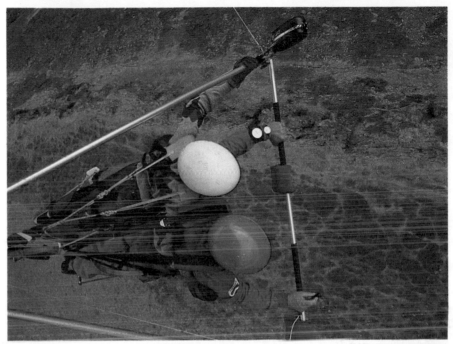

In-flight dual: the passenger's arm is around the pilot so both move in unison

The Japanese make some fine hang gliders. Yoshiki Oka with the Falhawk Cruiser 170

Competition Tasks: The development of decision making

In the early days tasks were simple:

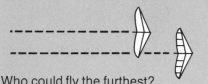

Who could fly the furthest?

or

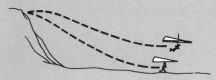

Who could stay in the air longest?

Then came landing accuracy, maybe coupled with points for duration as well:

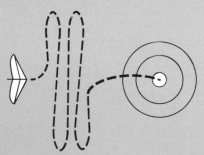

The so-called 'duration and spot' task was devised, which has continued to this day. Really only useful when there is no lift available, or to please a crowd.

When soaring is easy, duration tasks mean little, so speed range tests began:

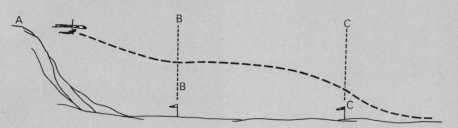

e.g. Fly as fast as possible from A to B, then remain in the air as long as possible between B and C. The decisions required are quite subtle: the winner will have judged the best compromise when trading off height for speed between A and B.

Unfortunately all these relatively simple contests are only fair if the wind is steady and the air stable. That condition is not normal, so tasks were devised which required pilots to exploit thermal lift, and the whole scale of competition changed:

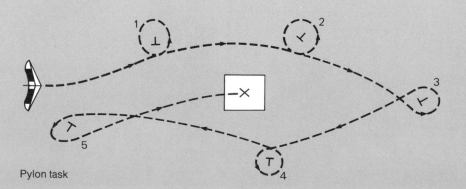

Pylon task

The pylon task is almost infinitely variable. In our example the pylons all have to be rounded in an anti-clockwise direction, but different rules may just as well apply. For a flight to score at all, the landing must be within the square. Possibly pylons 1 and 2 are in ridge lift, but a large gap may exist between 2 and 3, so that thermal assistance is required to reach the latter. After each pylon the pilots must assess the likelihood of rounding the next. As a test of skill, judgement and confidence the pylon task can be good: bear in mind when considering the variables, that the pilot achieving the greatest number of pylons wins, but in the event of a pylon-tie the winner is judged on speed.

As performance improved, the pylon task exhibited one serious shortcoming: it was almost impossible to identify a glider thousands of feet up in the sky, and it was equally difficult for the pilot to know with certainty that he had rounded a pylon. Hang gliders soon followed the example of their sailplane brethren and resorted to using photographic evidence of turn points. The scope immediately widened. No longer was an army of observers and marshals required: dog-leg courses to distant goals could be set. The 1984 XC Classic in the Owens Valley in California demanded flights which would have been as inconceivable to the competitors of a decade before as Concorde to the Wright Brothers.

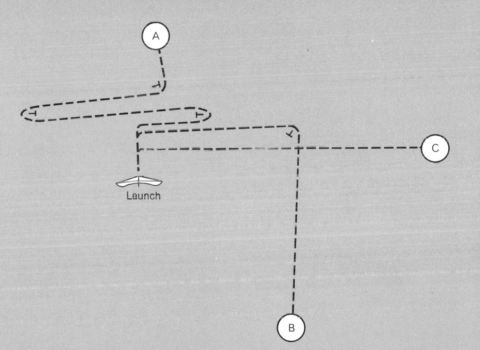

The 'classic' tasks
The decision-making is formidable. The rules allow pilots to attempt any route on each competition day: the choice is theirs. If they think conditions are unsuitable, then they don't fly—but that again is their decision.

After achieving the three different goals, competitors can repeat the tasks on subsequent days, to try and improve their times. Shortest time for the maximum number of goals wins. The goals are all about the same flight distance from launch. That distance is *one hundred miles*!

Task setting has indeed had to develop alongside glider performance.

When launching into a high wind it is essential that the pilot gets his weight well forward to maintain speed at launch. Len Hull taking off into a 30 mph (48 kph) wind

Competition flying

Background

If there were only two hang gliders in the world, sooner or later there would probably be a competition: someone would want to know which had the better performance or which pilot had the greater skills.

The first contests were either a test of glide angle (who could land the furthest out from a given hill) or duration (who could stay up longest). When the performance of the glider was such that distance

Competition: waiting to launch

was measured in feet and duration in seconds, such competitions were easy to run and reasonably fair to all concerned. Soon though, sink rate and controllability increased to the point where more selective tasks were required, tasks which usually combined two different elements of performance such as duration and landing accuracy or duration and speed.

These tasks are still flown, and serve a useful purpose, but glider performance has improved so much since the mid-1970s that competitions which explore cross-country potential are now common.

It has sometimes been difficult to keep up with the speed of development of both gliders and

contests, in which the technology of the aircraft designers has to be countered by the wiles of meet directors. Notably successful in this field has been Don Partridge, whose foresight in setting massive tasks in the daunting Owens Valley area on the California/Nevada border has led to regular performances of a standard which would have qualified as world records only a year earlier. In the eastern United States, Chattanooga's annual 'Great Race' along Lookout Mountain was also ahead of its time. This is a 23-mile ridge run along tree-covered slopes in Georgia and Tennessee, and was one of the first events to be run as a speed run pure and simple over a fixed course. In Europe, Sepp Himburger of Kössen in Austria had the acumen to see that hang gliding was a sport that could bring trade to the ski-lifts out of season, and organised an unofficial World Championship as far back as 1975. The significant step forward in Britain came with Brian Milton's innovation of a National League in which the top pilots competed against each other on a regular basis throughout the year. In a very short time the standard of both fliers and gliders rose beyond measure.

Starting in competition
Most clubs run some form of event from time to time, and of course

these are the ones to start in. It is impossible to recommend flying techniques for every possible task, but you can take some simple precautions which should ensure that you do not come last. The most obvious, yet most frequently overlooked, is to understand the rules thoroughly. It is just no use setting off with a vague idea of where you have to fly and what you have to do. Then, be sure your flight scores. For example, if the task is to

Steve Moyes, 1983 World Champion, on approach below the Tegelberg. Glider: Moyes 'Bullet'

An exciting scene as competition pilots launch under classic fluffy cumulus clouds

Typical competition tasks

1 Free distance

The name of this competition is really self-explanatory. The winner is the one who flies the greatest straight-line distance from the launch, other places being awarded in descending order. However, scoring can become complicated where the task is just one round in a longer event. The usual system is then to award a number of points to the winner of the round, say 300; everybody else's distances are expressed as a percentage of this. For example:

Winner covers 50 miles
=300 points

2nd place covers 25 miles
= *50 per cent of 50*
=150 points

3rd place covers 10 miles
=*20 per cent of 50*
=60 points

So far so good, but nobody ever flies nice round figures, so a pocket calculator begins to be an asset. Also our third-place man above would probably feel a little aggrieved, because although he only managed ten miles he may have beaten another forty competitors on the day. Maybe by an almost superhuman effort he managed to stretch his glide across

fly around as many pylons as possible before landing in a designated area, then it is far better for the novice to clear two pylons and land near the target than to get round three but find himself landing out for a zero.

One form of contest which is open to any member of the BHGA is the annual Cross-Country, or XC, League. Whereas the National League is an intense competition circuit with a very select membership which now meets about five time a season, the XC League is a register of the best three cross-country flights any pilot records during the year. There are three categories in which to enter: free distance, out-and-return and

triangle flight. The fee is extremely small and the winner holds a beautiful handmade 'Eagle' trophy donated by XC League mastermind David Harrison.

The top seventy-five entries are published month by month in the BHGA's magazine, *Wings*! and it is really interesting to be able to plot your progress against the performance of some of the 'big names'. Invitations to join the National League are based on performance in the XC League. As British team selection is made virtually exclusively from National League fliers, there is a clear route open for any committed pilot to work his way up to contests at International level.

a river and into the next field to beat a larger group. His reward for this could be 60 points while many of the rest get 59.9! Simply to overcome this objection we complicate the job still further. In our typical round we will say 200 distance points and 100 for position. To keep the example simple we will assume an entry of fifty fliers. Thus:

Winner covers 50 miles
—300 points as before
(*200 distance + 100 position*)

2nd place covers 25 miles
(*50 per cent*) =198 points
(*100 distance + 98 position*)

3rd place covers 10 miles
(*20 per cent*) =136 points
(*40 distance + 96 position*)

It can be seen that the distance points are allotted as a percentage of the winner's distance, while each position in our example is worth 2 points (50 entries = 100 position points available).

The result is rather fairer than before. Our third-place man may still complain that he is hard done by, but he will not grumble half as much as he did in example 1.

Competition: a fiercely fought ridge race in progress

2 Ridge race
This task may be scored in two ways, according to the conditions. If the ridge is obviously soarable all the way to the turn point and back, then normally each competitor is simply timed from takeoff to finish, and his elapsed time is the basis for his score. However, if conditions are marginal and thermal assistance will be needed to fly the course, then the task may be scored on a 'first home' basis.

The latter method opens up tremendous scope for gamesmanship. Normally it works like this: the competition director declares a 'launch window'—that is,

Inspection

Assessment

Preparation

Attack

Launched

Into first turn

US team flyer Rich Pfeiffer executes a classic launch sequence in a Wills Wing 'Duck'

Stretching the glide to reach a target. Glider: 'Firebird'

a time when anyone can take off. This may be quite long, such as 10.00 am to 2.00 pm. It is up to the individual competitor when he starts, and of course it is a great test of judgement. Does he go early and risk 'going down', or is it better to play safe as far as completing the task is concerned, but be beaten by a more daring soul prepared to gamble on finding enough lift?

Scoring may be directly in relation to finishing order, or a variation of the percentage method outlined in task 1 may be applied.

It is worth noting that in a well-run competition all speed tasks and races should be timed to the crossing of a line, while the pilot is still airborne. It is obviously dangerous if the time of touchdown is taken. Competitors should not be put in a position where diving at the ground to save a few seconds will benefit anyone.

Events which are timed from takeoff to impact are likely to get the sport a bad name!

3 Duration and spot
Still a popular task for light-wind days, or to entertain the public. The pilot must stay aloft as long as possible before landing in a target area. Usually there is a limit applied to the duration—maybe an hour—beyond which the score for the task cannot be enhanced.

Points for the event are awarded

Ian Jarman (Australia) uses his body-drag to steepen glide approach to a target. Glider: Moyes 'Missile'

Tony Hughes jubilantly displays the magnificent trophy he earned by winning the prestigious 1983 Cross Country Classic Competition in the USA

131

The pilot of this Hiway 'Demon' makes an old monument his turn point

Photographing a turn point

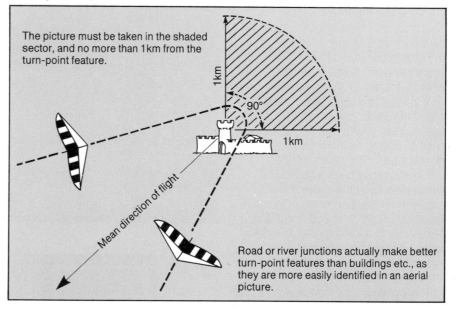

The picture must be taken in the shaded sector, and no more than 1km from the turn-point feature.

1km

90°

1km

Mean direction of flight

Road or river junctions actually make better turn-point features than buildings etc., as they are more easily identified in an aerial picture.

A typical task-board to be photographed before starting

LEAGUE 4

TASK No.

3

23·8·84

One of the last chores before a competition pilot launches is often to take a picture of the task identification board. Pilots: Johnny Carr and Mark Southall

for time in the air, and lost according to distance from the bull's-eye. It has been known for conditions to improve during the flying of this task to the extent that all competitors stay up for the maximum duration, in which case the only meaningful part of the score becomes that of landing accuracy.

4 Pylon task
If this conjures up a picture of hang gliders scraping their wingtips around something normally used to support high-tension wires, now is the time to revise your impression.

In hang gliding competitions, a pylon is usually a tripod three or four feet high supporting a horizontal mirror plus a sighting ring. By looking into the mirror, the observer can see whether the competitor has correctly rounded the turn point marked beside him by a flag.

In a pylon task a number of these are set up at varying distances from the launch. Each will have apportioned to it a number of points, often increasing according to how difficult it is to reach.

Scoring is usually on the basis of pylon points plus elapsed time points, from which you can see that this is a real decision-making task. Should you gamble on successfully clearing a distant pylon but taking a long time in so doing, or will it be better to scream off and round just

the nearest one as quickly as possible? If conditions allow nobody to get around pylon two, then you guessed right by going just for the nearest and won the task, but if just one flier made the second, then you blew it!

5 XC to designated goals
In some ways this is similar to the pylon task, and poses the same type of challenge. The goals may be very long distances apart and present a great test of piloting skill. Of course they will probably not be in a straight line, so do you set off with the aim of going direct to the furthest, or is it better to keep your options open by setting a course for the nearest and going on from there if you have sufficient height? As with all tasks where choices are presented, the winner will be the pilot who can combine fine judgement of the weather conditions with outstanding flying skill.

6 'One on one'
In contests with a reasonable number of rounds the so-called 'one on one' scoring system has a lot going for it. Each pilot is paired against one other, and the result is decided simply on his sum total of wins and losses. Obviously the pairings are changed in each round, and usually spot landings are required in some tasks, but these

are used only as tie-breakers.

The system has little support in Britain, but is quite popular in the USA where it seems to work well.

Cameras and competition

As cross-country tasks grow more and more ambitious, photographic evidence of the course is becoming very important. Pilots are commonly asked to fly to a turn point and then go for maximum distance, or go out and return, and a photograph will have to be taken of the appropriate ground features to prove that the turn was correctly made. Sometimes the organisers will specify the type of camera (e.g. 126 or 110) to fit in with the film-processing arrangements, or alternatively you provide your own. Whichever is the case, you can take certain elementary steps to avoid disappointing failure: if you have to provide the camera, do not go out and buy one on the day of the contest—get it a week or two before and run a film through to be sure it works. Whatever else, tie the camera to either you or the glider with a lanyard of some sort. A lanyard can look exactly like a piece of string. Do try out the camera when wearing the gloves you fly in, and be sure that you can operate the film-transport mechanism

Camera dangling, French Champion Gerard Thevenot completes a 360° among the mountains. Glider: La Mouette 'Profil'

Photographing a turn point

It is not enough to take any old shot of a turn point. To prove that you have done the task correctly, the photograph must be taken from a point beyond the turn feature. The FAI requirements are basically that the picture is taken while the competitor is not more than 1 km from the turn point, and in the 90° sector diametrically opposite the mean direction of the course.

Records

For many participants the holding of a world or national record is the pinnacle of achievement in their chosen sport.

The rules for these records are made by the FAI, and claims will not be accepted unless they are made absolutely according to the rules.

In Britain, the BHGA acts as the clearing house for claims, and will assist with information, but it is up to the individual pilot to ensure that he is familiar with the current requirements of the FAI sporting code.

The flights for which world or national records may be claimed are:

Distance   A flight without turn points from a takeoff place to a landing place, measured in a straight line.

(wind-on) without any difficulty.

Virtually any camera of 35 mm or less will serve, unless you are specifically after records, in which case it must take cartridge film and have no rewind facility.

Avoid the very smallest because they are too fiddly to use with gloves on, and avoid anything boasting a telephoto lens. A camera advertised as suitable for underwater or rugged use should be ideal, bearing in mind the treatment it is likely to receive, and the weather it must endure. If your flying progresses to record-breaking levels, the camera becomes very important indeed.

Cliff launch for an intermediate pilot. Note the nose-down attitude before takeoff. Unusually nowadays the flier still prefers to fly seated. Glider: Goldmarque 'Gyr'

Distance to goal This is measured to a previously declared goal.

Out and return From takeoff to a turn point and back past takeoff site. Photographic evidence of the turn point and return to launch are now acceptable. It is not necessary to actually land at the launch point—obviously this would be impractical at most mountain sites.

Height gain Overall height climbed, as measured on a barograph, from low to high points during a flight. This means that if you sink below takeoff height the actual height subsequently gained is measured, not just the height above takeoff.

There are two classes of hang glider recognised for which records may be claimed: those with flexible surfaces and controlled exclusively by pilot weight shift, and those with rigid airfoils and/or pilot-actuated aerodynamic controls. In addition to the general category, records may also be claimed for the best performance by a woman pilot, and the best performance with more than one person aboard. In the latter category, any passengers carried must have an all-up weight of at least 75 kg complete with parachute, harness etc.

Record claimants must hold an FAI sporting licence, obtainable through the national body at modest cost. Apart from that the evidence required is logical but sometimes complex, so check, check and check again. Full requirements are listed in the BHGA Observer handbook.

One of the beauties of our sport is that once you have progressed beyond the beginner stage you will come into contact with advanced fliers as a matter of course. Unlike more formalised activities where the aces train alone, you are quite likely to be sharing the hillside with world-class competitors. Anyone with the wit to learn by example and the common sense not to push himself too hard will in turn become an advanced flier in due course.

Pilot three

The advancing pilot will rapidly build up the flying experience enabling him to attain Pilot 3 status. The actual flying requirements are not very difficult, but the written examination calls for quite a lot of study from various sources. The holder of a P3 may justly claim to be an advanced pilot.

Pilot 3 requirements

Before applying for a Pilot 3 rating the pilot must have held a Pilot 2 rating for at least four months.

Tasks 1 and 2 may be attempted before having completed the Pilot 2 task form.

1 High Altitude
The pilot must:
a. make one flight during which the terrain clearance exceeds 300 metres (1,000 ft) for at least ten minutes. Well co-ordinated 720° turns must be accomplished in both directions.
b. have flown at altitudes exceeding 200 metres, for a minimum of ten minutes' duration out of ridge lift and displaying good thermalling techniques.

2 Duration
The pilot must:
a. make five one-hour soaring flights, at least two being prone or supine, from a minimum of three different sites.
b. have 25 hours logged flying time on hang gliders. At least half these must be completed on a high-performance hang glider.

3 Cross-country
The pilot must:
a. make three cross-country distance flights of at least 10, 20 and 30 kilometres between takeoff and landing.

b. be able to explain and discuss in detail how he would cope with the following problems:
i. The determination of upper and lower wind directions from natural sources, while in flight.
ii. The setting up of conservative planned approaches to unfamiliar landing areas and the allowance of a sufficient margin of error for unexpected changes in circumstances.
iii. Wind, turbulence, shear and lift conditions in various regions, such as valleys, mountains, built-up and wooded areas.

4 Precision flying
The pilot must:
a. demonstrate and discuss three top landing methods (subject to site conditions).
b. demonstrate the various forms of 360° and 720° turns exhibiting precise control and co-ordination, both in and out of lift.

5 Theoretical requirements
The pilot must pass a BHGA written examination on Air Law, Navigation, Meteorology, and Principles of Flight.

The detailed requirements for Pilot 2 and Pilot 3 are likely to change in 1985, but the overall flying standard will be unaltered.

Cameras and hang gliders

The combination of blue skies, sun, brightly coloured fabric wings and the sometimes bizarre outfits of the harnessed pilots, make hang gliding a target for the lenses of many camera owners. Unfortunately the results are often disappointing and serve only to boost the trade of film manufacturers and photo processing business.

Here are some tips for inexperienced photographers which should save a few wasted frames.

A. Filming from the ground
1. If your camera incorporates an automatic exposure meter—and most do these days—remember that a subject such as a hang glider will often be under-exposed when shot against a bright sky. Compensate by pre-setting the exposure against a more averagely-lit subject such as the hillside and then take the picture of the glider.
2. Be prepared to be disappointed by shots of gliders which are supposed to show how amazingly high up they are. You will end up with a picture which may as well be of bats, mosquitos or even dirt on the lens! The best hang-gliding shots are usually taken with the aircraft no more than fifty feet (18 m) from the ground, and with some ground features incorporated to give a sense of scale.
3. If photographing take-off action, don't be afraid of getting in close—always provided you are out of range of the wingtip. Not every picture has to contain the complete glider to be effective. It also helps to talk to the pilot first: he will tell you when he plans to launch and if you are likely to be in the way. Most pilots are very approachable, but don't interrupt their pre-flight routine checks.
4. Do be aware of the background. A glider just above the horizon will make a better picture than one just below.
5. Don't imagine that because you do not have an elaborate camera and a battery of different lenses you cannot take pictures of hang gliding. Some of the pictures in this book have been taken through very expensive Zeiss lenses while others were made via a battered Olympus Trip 35 pocket camera. I don't think anyone would be able to identify all the latter with certainty.

One of the BHGA's test rigs being used to check the pitch stability of an older glider. The camera records the scene as towing starts. The two standing observers read out the wind speed while the seated engineer measures the forces on the control bar. (Approx. 1/250th at f5.6, 50 mm lens)

6. Think of the sun. West-facing sites are best for moody sunset shots. Midday pictures often disappoint because the pilot is always in shadow from the wing and thus appears rather dark. At other times try and anticipate when the glider will turn so that the light illuminates the undersurface to give shape and texture to the form of the wing.

B. Filming in the air

The taking of record shots for competition purposes is covered elsewhere, but the pilot who wants to communicate the flavour and excitement of hang gliding will be seeking higher quality. Again a little thought and trouble can greatly improve the results.

1. Do not try in-flight photography until you can fly confidently and safely, and always be aware of other fliers on the hill.

2. Pick a camera with a relatively wide-angle lens—say 35 mm or less on a 35 mm film camera. If you focus it to about 6 ft (2 m) and use quite a small aperture, you can be sure that everything you take will be in sharp focus.

3. If taking hand-held shots, try and operate the shutter during a turn, and so that a wingtip comes into the corner of the frame. This gives depth to the picture. If you can get the rigging area with a few parked gliders into the shot, so much the better. And finally, a bit of sky as well as hillside or ground adds space and position.

4. Again, think of the sun. Shots of a hillside in shadow will usually be less rewarding than those where the sun is highlighting the detail.

5. If vanity gets the better of you, and you decide to mount the camera remotely so that you the pilot are in the picture, then do the

job carefully and safely. A remote control is necessary, and the electric variety is more reliable than the pneumatic type, assuming that your camera will accept one. An appropriate balance weight is important, especially where the camera is mounted towards a wingtip. Do not attempt to fly if the static balance of the glider feels awkward before take-off, and be ready for aerodynamic drag while flying. Also, beware of 'lash-up' arrangements. Cameras and balance weights tied on with string or tape are potentially lethal to both pilot and the spectators below.

6. It is worth taking the trouble to tape the remote shutter wire out of sight behind the control frame tubes and to lead it along inside the sail where possible, so avoiding distracting wires in shot.

7. If your camera, still or cine, uses a 'through the lens' viewfinder system, then cover up the eyepiece with a piece of black tape before flying. This tip eliminates that bright ring which often appears on amateur films and slides.

8. Generally speaking, the wider the angle of the lens, the better, although ultra-wide 'fisheye' shots become very repetitive after a while.

9. If attempting remote-controlled in-flight shots, be prepared to use quite a lot of film, and discard all but the very best exposures. Obviously a camera with some sort of power wind-on is virtually essential because the alternative of one shot per flight greatly reduces the chance of success. And don't forget to switch the camera on before take-off!

8. Powered hang gliding and towing

It is true that few sporting experiences can compare with that of launching a hang glider from a steep hill—but this is small comfort if you have no access to suitable hills. It is not surprising that there have been many experiments with methods of taking off from flat fields.

If the object of the exercise is to gain sufficient height to search for thermals as a basis for soaring flight, then a truly safe and effective method has so far eluded the experimenters. Work continues, and will no doubt bear fruit in due course, but an appreciation of the problems will be useful for the adventurous pilot.

Len Gabriels with his early keel-mounted power system. He flew this aircraft from north of London to Abbeville in France one day in August 1979. Glider: Skyhook 'Safari'

Power

Because only about 5 or 6 bhp are required to sustain a hang glider in level flight, it appears to be a simple matter to attach a small motor of the type used in chainsaws or lightweight motorcycles. Geared to a suitable propeller such a power unit does indeed produce sufficient thrust, but a number of difficulties also appear: most obvious is that wherever the motor is fitted it is likely to be in the way of the pilot, or to produce a dangerous thrustline.

The very earliest power attachments, described as 'glide

Hiway 160 Skytrike powering a rare Birdman Comanche wing

extenders' right back in the days of the old standard Rogallo kites, consisted of a small motor driving a fan-type prop, all of which was encased in a wire cage and strapped to the seated pilot's back, rucksack style. As the performance of the gliders themselves was very poor and the pilot's body almost completely blanketed the small propellor, these backpack attachments never did much more than make a noise, and did not become popular. However, because the thrustline was low and the centre of mass remained well below the wing, they did not introduce any stability problems, which is more than can be said for their successors.

The next step was to attach the motor towards the front of the glider's keel just beneath the sail, and drive a propeller at the tail via a long shaft. These attachments worked quite well, and pilots such as Gerry Breen and Len Gabriels made some long and heroic flights on aircraft of this type. The big difficulty was that of control in turbulence, or more specifically, lack of it. The high thrustline meant that if the pilot became temporarily weightless, as often happens in rough air, pendular stability was lost and it was easy for the wing to be pitched up into a stall or powered down in such a way as to invert with astonishing rapidity. Even the

adoption of mouth-operated throttles, allowing the engine to be cut instantly in emergency, was not enough to ensure the safety of high thrustline glider-mounted systems.

Add relatively minor irritations such as the ability of a small two-stroke engine to spray substantial quantities of unburned oil over the sail, chronic lack of mechanical reliability and the propeller's unfortunate tendency to mutilate the pilot's feet in the event of a crash landing, and it is easy to see why these devices enjoyed at best a limited popularity.

The final nail in the coffin for engines mounted directly on the wing came with the introduction of the 'trike' unit early in 1980. These wheeled seats with an engine mounted behind the pilot, and suspended via a universal joint at the glider's hangpoint, have proved most successful as a system for powering a hang glider wing into the air. Unfortunately, the added weight and drag so degrade the glide performance that the original aim of climbing up and cutting the power in favour of thermal soaring is generally impractical. Instead the trike has developed into a separate form of aircraft in its own right, and is more correctly dealt with in a companion volume *The Complete Microlight Guide*.

Hang gliding experience is invaluable for flying microlight

aircraft, and the CAA will grant a microlight Private Pilot's Licence (PPL Group 'D') to holders of a BHGA Pilot 2 Certificate after only 5 hours powered training. The normal requirement is 15 hours.

In the USA several different types of rigid-winged hang glider, notably the 'Easy Riser' and 'Quicksilver' were the basis for added power. The end product, although looking rather different, was the same as in Britain: the aircraft soon acquired wheels, strengthening, instruments, cockpit enclosure—and lots of extra weight! More power became essential to hoist it all into the sky and so the aeroplane was re-invented. The original aim of a simple clip-on power booster as a soaring aid was lost, although the technology learned in hang gliding undoubtedly aided the growth of the microlight industry.

In the UK, any powered aircraft weighing more than 70 kg must be registered by the CAA, and increasingly onerous airworthiness requirements must be met. As the microlight movement becomes more and more regulated and the designs move ever closer to the field of orthodox light aviation, the time must now be right for another wave of attempts at very lightweight add-on power systems to keep the end product under the critical 70 kg figure.

Towing

The sight of sailplanes being towed from a flat field is very familiar, and it may appear surprising that few hang glider pilots attempt it. The problem is that towing has proven rather hazardous for a variety of reasons, and none of the methods tried so far has been completely satisfactory.

All tow systems call for a very high level of skill on the part of both pilot and ground crew. The degree of control which the pilot can exert is limited, and if the rate of tow is too fast the glider can become pitched up and in effect 'power stalled'. Alternatively a control 'lock out' may occur in which the glider accelerates rapidly sideways like a child's kite with stability problems. In either case the weight of the pilot cannot effectively be employed to counteract the forces in play. Even if he is able to release at once from the tow, the glider may very well whip-stall, then spin or tuck. There seems to be more danger from 'lock up' than 'lock out', as it is extremely difficult for an observer to assess the angle of attack from the towing vehicle or winch, whereas any sideways deviation is immediately apparent.

Towing is a very specialised field, and a brief description of various systems is included here so that the ambitious pilot can better judge what to avoid rather than how to do it! This may be unfair to the latest methods of 'body' or 'harness' towing, which are quite promising.

The simplest systems, which go back to the days of flat-kite towing in water-ski shows, use a fixed length of rope joined via a link to the tow vehicle. At the glider end the towrope branches into a 'Y', each arm of which terminates in a quick-release coupling operated via cables from bicycle-brake type levers on the control bar. One quick-release is near the top of the control frame, and the other in the centre of the bar. The separate releases are to control the climb rate, the upper one being disengaged once the glider is safely off the ground, whereupon towing continues via the lower. This way a skilled pilot with a good crew can get almost vertically above the tow vehicle. A variation of this scheme uses not one but two lower connections, one at each end of the control bar.

The 'Trike' system became the safest and most popular method of powering a hang glider. Glider: Solar Typhoon 'S'. Trike Hiway 250cc

The problems

Apart from the 'lock-out' possibilities, there are mechanical difficulties: the control frame must be reinforced to withstand the extra loads. The release mechanisms must eject the towrope cleanly from any angle which may be reached, especially if the glider should overrun the tow vehicle. On systems where two levers are used, the pilot must pull them in the correct order. Not, you may think, a particularly challenging task, but

The old style of towing. Note the twin release levers on the bar. Glider: Super Scorpion

quite easy to perform incorrectly at the learning stage. It was to overcome this problem that a single lever system demanding to be pulled twice was devised, but on some of these a mechanical shortcoming occasionally allowed them to eject both tow points simultaneously.

Fixed towing methods always introduce the possibility of destroying the glider in the air by imposing excessive loads upon the airframe. The tow driver must understand this and be able to judge conditions perfectly. He must always have an experienced observer with him who never takes his eyes off the pilot. 'Weak-links' of known breaking strain are often incorporated into the towrope to avoid overload, but the violent release they involve can also lead to a stall.

These fixed towing methods are now used almost exclusively on water, and for 'tow vehicle' read 'boat'. It is generally accepted that fixed towing over land is too dangerous, and is actively discouraged.

Marginally safer are winch systems, because a constant-load clutch can be incorporated to control the tow. However, they demand a substantial capital outlay and meticulous maintenance, and so work on their development is still slow.

Exhibition towing behind a boat at Cypress Gardens, Florida

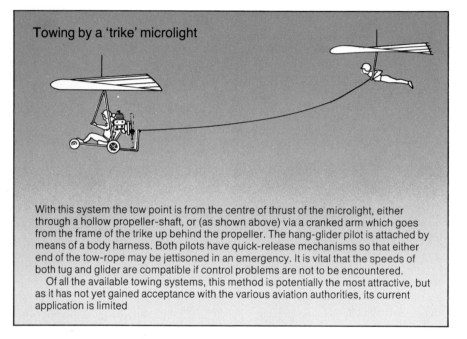

Towing by a 'trike' microlight

With this system the tow point is from the centre of thrust of the microlight, either through a hollow propeller-shaft, or (as shown above) via a cranked arm which goes from the frame of the trike up behind the propeller. The hang-glider pilot is attached by means of a body harness. Both pilots have quick-release mechanisms so that either end of the tow-rope may be jettisoned in an emergency. It is vital that the speeds of both tug and glider are compatible if control problems are not to be encountered.

Of all the available towing systems, this method is potentially the most attractive, but as it has not yet gained acceptance with the various aviation authorities, its current application is limited

The current trend among towing enthusiasts is to tow from a point on the pilot's harness, about halfway between his shoulders and the hang-point. Variations abound—in some a yoke is fitted between harness and glider, the towrope release being fixed to the apex. By altering the length of the yoke legs, the proportion of pulling effort can be adjusted between glider and pilot until the best compromise is found.

These systems may one day become popular as a way of bringing hang gliding to flat lands, and although some are available commercially in the USA and Europe, the truly definitive method will not emerge until much more experience has been gained in widely differing conditions.

No pilot should embark upon towing experiments without talking to some of the old hands in the business. Signalling systems must be worked out in advance, and must be foolproof: the pilot has no free hands with which to wave, and leg movements are very easily misinterpreted in the air!

The tow pilot at this time needs a rare blend of courage and caution, plus a highly developed understanding of the foul-up factor!

9. Rules, regulations and recommendations

Don't let this rather daunting heading put you off. Hang gliding is by far the most free form of flying, but like it or not we are still bound by the Air Navigation Order, as is any other aviator in the UK. The subject is enormous, but fortunately we are directly affected by only a small section of it, and almost exclusively in the interests of the safety of ourselves and others. Much fuller details will be found in various CAA and BHGA publications, and it is the responsibility of the pilot to know his air law. Here are a few of the basics in as far as they affect a pilot just out of training school:

Pedestrians must keep clear of the 'flight lane' at the Tegelberg landing site

Some general flying rules

1 A glider shall not be operated in a reckless or negligent manner so as to endanger life or property, nor flown in such proximity to another aircraft as to create a danger of collision, nor in formation without prior agreement of the pilots.
2 No person shall be drunk in the aircraft.
3 Nothing shall be dropped from a glider other than persons by parachute in an emergency, articles for life saving or ballast in the form of fine sand or water.
4 Aircraft not equipped for instrument flying must only be operated in Visual Meteorological Conditions (VMC). That means all hang gliders at present and for the foreseeable future.

Collision avoidance rules

1 If meeting another aircraft head-on, turn away to the RIGHT. Obviously if this happens close to a ridge, only the glider with the ridge on its left is able to turn.
2 If two aircraft are flying in the same direction, but on converging courses, that with the other on its RIGHT must give way.
3 When overtaking, pass on the RIGHT. However, beware of an

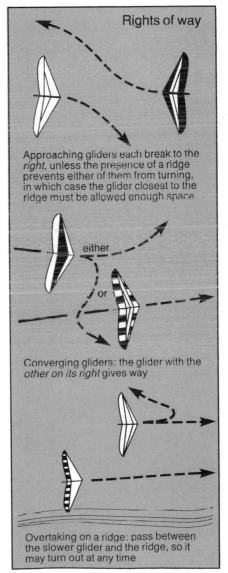

Rights of way

Approaching gliders each break to the *right*, unless the presence of a ridge prevents either of them from turning, in which case the glider closest to the ridge must be allowed enough space

either

or

Converging gliders: the glider with the *other on its right* gives way

Overtaking on a ridge: pass between the slower glider and the ridge, so it may turn out at any time

145

exception to this law, which requires that when ridge soaring the overtaking glider must pass between the ridge and the glider being overtaken. This is so that the slower glider is not 'penned in' and can turn away from the hill at any time.

4 When two aircraft are at differing heights, the *lower* has priority. This is especially important when on landing approach.

5 It is the duty of all pilots at all times to fly in such a manner as to avoid collision.

BHGA flying regulations

1 A well-fitting helmet must be worn on all flights.

2 A hang glider shall not be flown from any site without first obtaining permission from the landowner, or club, or school official in charge of site arrangements.

3 A hang glider shall not be flown unless it has been inspected after rigging and is in an airworthy condition. The pilot is responsible for checking the glider that he is going to fly.

4 A hang glider shall not be flown unless its pilot is covered by 3rd party insurance to a value accepted by BHGA (£500,000 in 1982).

5 A glider joining another in a thermal shall be circled in the same

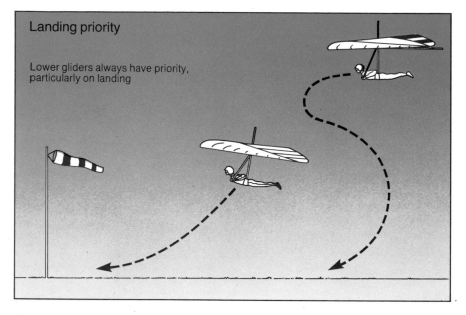

Landing priority

Lower gliders always have priority, particularly on landing

direction as that established by the first.

BGHA flying recommendations

1 Never fly alone. There should always be someone on the ground on site concerned with your welfare. If there are just two of you and you are both flying, avoid losing sight of each other. Always tell some responsible person where you intend to fly and at what time you intend to return home. Never leave another pilot flying alone.

2 Avoid going into cloud. It is easy to become disorientated, and, if you lose control, to overstress the glider so that it breaks. If low orographic cloud starts forming near the hill land at once. If cu-nimbs (thunder clouds) are growing and the lift is strong leave the thermal *at least* 600 ft (200 m) below cloud.

3 Do not modify a hang glider or a harness unless the manufacturer agrees to the changes. Do not adjust or tune a hang glider without following the manufacturer's instructions or getting assistance from a person known to have the necessary technical knowledge and skill.

4 Do not experiment with towing, winching or motorised hang gliding without first obtaining technical advice and information from BHGA.
5 When soaring cross country or in wave it is advisable to carry a parachute and to know how to use it.
6 Avoid flying if you have been drinking or if you have a hangover. If prescribed drugs, check with the doctor about any effects such as drowsiness. *Never* mix drinks and drugs.

Code of good practice

The site
a. When seeking permission to fly from a landowner, occupier or controlling authority, always present your BHGA and Club membership cards. State exactly where you wish to fly and where you intend to land.
b. When visiting a site administered by another Club, *always* contact it in advance and observe local rules.
c. All soaring sites should now be known to the Military Air Traffic Organisation. Pilots of low flying aircraft are briefed to avoid sites at weekends. Please report any new soaring site to the BHGA office so that MATO can be informed.
d. If your flying activities are likely to cause traffic congestion please inform the local Police.
e. Designate the takeoff, landing and rigging areas. Keep these free

from spectators and parked hang gliders.
f. Do not leave a rigged hang glider unattended and always park into the wind.
g. Avoid all standing crops. If you should land in them, minimise your movements and get out with as little damage as possible.
h. Always report any damage (however small) to the landowner.

Animals
a. Avoid all livestock. If they tend to migrate to one area, try to avoid disturbing them there.
b. Do not fly from a site where livestock are about to bear their young, (e.g. lambing, calving and having foals.) This is usually the late February to May period and varies with the breed and locality. Check with the farmer if any livestock is likely to be startled.
c. Dogs should never be taken onto any site unless the landowner's permission has been obtained. They must be kept under control at all times.

Organisations and addresses

British

British Hang Gliding Association
(BHGA)
Cranfield Airfield
Cranfield
Bedfordshire
MK43 0YR
Tel: Bedford (0234) 751688

Civil Aviation Authority (CAA)
CAA House
45–59 Kingsway
London
WC2B 6TE

International

Fédération Aeronautique
Internationale (FAI)
6 rue Gaililee
75782 Paris
France

Hang gliding matters are dealt with
by:
Commission Internationale du Vol
Libre (CIVL) at the FAI address
above.

Further reading

Bob Mackay, *An Introduction to Hang Gliding*, Thornhill Press

Dennis Pagen, *Hang Gliding Flying Skills*, Dennis Pagen (USA)

Dennis Pagen, *Meteorology for Hang Glider Pilots*, Dennis Pagen (USA)

Dennis Pagen, *Hang Gliding Techniques*, Dennis Pagen (USA)

Dan Poynter, *Hang Gliding*, Dan Poynter Publications (USA)

Ann Welch, *KTG Hang Gliding*, A & C Black

Ann Welch & Roy Hill, *Soaring Hang Gliders*, John Murray

George Worthington, *In Search of World Records*, San Diego Hang Gliding Press (USA)

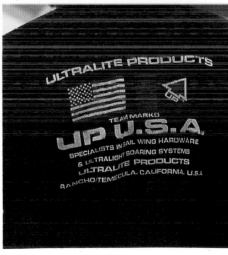

The colour and sights of a beautiful sport

Glossary of terms

Aerofoil (airfoil) The shape of the section of a wing.

Angle of attack The angle at which the *aerofoil* enters the airflow.

ASI Airspeed indicator.

Aspect ratio (A/R) The span of the wing divided by the average *chord*.

Back-up Safety system; typically a second hang-loop or a parachute.

Batten Metal, plastic or glass-fibre insert which defines the aerofoil section and stiffens the sail.

Billow The amount of slackness in the sail after it has been fitted to the airframe. Virtually non-existent on high-performance designs.

Blob Small area of thermal lift.

Boomer Very strong thermal.

Bottle screw Device employing left- and right-handed threads to adjust the length of a rigging wire.

CFX Concealed Floating Crossboom glider.

Chord The distance between the leading and trailing edge of a wing.

Clag Low cloud, or any other cause of poor visibility.

Crab Karabiner: the clip which connects the harness to the glider.

De-flexor Strut supporting an extra rigging wire controlling the flexing of major tube in the airframe— usually the leading edge. Little used nowadays.

Flare-out The art of pushing the nose of the glider upwards so as to stall the wing and come to a halt at the correct height for landing.

Ground loop Being blown over backwards owing to careless ground handling. Alternatively, being spun round laterally through catching a wingtip on landing.

Hang loop Usually a fabric sling fitted close to the centre of gravity of the glider, to which the karabiner is attached. Also referred to as a 'hang point' in popular usage.

L/D Ratio of lift to drag. Provides a realistic indication of the glide angle attainable. The higher the ratio the flatter the glide.

Leech lines, or **luff lines** Cords which connect the trailing edge of the wing with the kingpost in order to maintain stabilising *reflex* in the sail.

Luffing dive A dive in which the pressure above the wing exceeds

that below: the aerofoil form is lost and the pilot has a genuine problem on his hands. Modern gliders incorporate many features to make the luffing dive an impossibility.

Min-sink (rate) The minimum rate at which the glider descends through the air; typically between 170 and 200 feet per minute (approximately 1 metre per second).

Min-sink (speed) The flying speed at which the glider's rate of descent is smallest.

Mylar Trade name for a very stable plastic sheeting used as a stiffener in sails.

Nonk Clumsy flier.

Over the falls Going thus is being ejected from a thermal in a nose-down attitude.

Pip pin A quick-release pin used in place of a bolt for ease of assembly.

Ragwing Any flexible-winged hang glider.

Reflex A slight upturn along the trailing edge of the wing which ensures that the glider cannot become stabilised in a dive.

Rogallo Term used to describe almost any hang glider using a delta configuration, named after Dr Francis M. Rogallo, whose experiments in the 1950s led to the modern flexwing.

Sailwing Early term for flexwing hang gliders.

Scratching Flying very close to the hill in order to maintain height in marginal lift. Risky for novices.

Skying out Soaring very high.

Specking out Soaring very high indeed.

Spoiler Movable flap which modifies the lift on the wing when operated. Used to induce and control roll on some rigid-wing gliders.

Sled ride A flight from top to bottom of a hill without encountering lift.

Stirrup loop Elastic loop through which the ankle is placed to facilitate locating the stirrup when airborne.

Tip stall When the tip of a wing ceases to develop sufficient lift to fly: this can lead to an uncontrollable spin into the hill or can present great difficulty when slowing down to land.

Tuck A violent and rapid forward inversion of the glider when flying. Normally the result of ill-judged aerobatics or radical turbulence.

Vario (variometer): instrument showing the rate of climb or sink.

Washout The twist in the wing which reduces the angle of attack towards the tips, and which is designed to prevent *tip stalls*.

XC Cross-country.

Gerhard Hölzenbein
Drachenflugschule

Index